FINGERPICK
J·S·BACH

by Marcel Robinson

FINGERPICKING
J·S·BACH

by Marcel Robinson

Amsco Publications
New York/London/Sydney

Book design by Katrina Orlowsky
Cover illustration by Pearce Marchbank.
Edited by Brook Hedick and Peter Pickow

Copyright © 1981 by Amsco Publications,
A Division of Music Sales Corporation, New York, NY.

All rights reserved. No part of this book may be
reproduced in any form or by any electronic or mechanical means
including information storage and retrieval systems,
without permission in writing from the publisher.

Order No.
US International Standard Book Number:
UK International Standard Book Number:

Exclusive Distributors:
Music Sales Corporation
257 Park Avenue South, New York, NY 10010 USA
Music Sales Limited
8/9 Frith Street, London W1V 5TZ England
Music Sales Pty. Limited
120 Rothschild Street, Rosebery, Sydney, NSW 2018, Australia

Printed in the United States of America by
Vicks Lithograph and Printing Corporation

Contents

Preface   7

Musette
from the Notenbuch vor Anna Magdalena Bach   8

Theme
from the Brandenburg Concerto No. 2 in F Major
  (*first movement*)   10

Minuet
from the Notenbuch vor Anna Magdalena Bach   12

March
from the Notenbuch vor Anna Magdalena Bach   14

Jesu, Joy of Man's Desiring
Jesu bleibet meine Freude *from Cantata No. 147*   16

Gavotte I and II
from the sixth Cello Suite   20

Sleepers Awake!
Wachet Auf *from Cantata No. 140*   24

O Sacred Head Now Wounded
O Haupt voll Blut und Wunden *from the* Passion according
  to Saint Matthew   28

Gavotte I and II
from the Orchestral Suite No. 3 in D Major   30

Bourree
from the first Lute Suite   35

Gavotte
from the third Lute Suite   39

Badinerie
from the Orchestral Suite No. 2 in B Minor   42

Preface

Johann Sebastian Bach (1685-1750) may well be the most beloved composer of all time: Have you ever met anyone who didn't like Bach's music? Throughout his prolific career he maintained a standard of excellence that has seldom, if ever, been equaled. It is this popularity coupled with this musical perfection that made the compilation of this book a delightful possibility.

In choosing the material for inclusion, we have tried to select works and excerpts that are familiar in addition to being suitable for transcription. Special care has been taken to retain the integrity of each original while making it accessible to this new audience of fingerstyle guitarists. The notation and symbols are all standard as we have used no "special effects." It is our hope that classical, folk, jazz, and rock guitarists alike will find this collection helpful for study as well as performance purposes.

Musette

from the Notenbuch vor Anna Magdalena Bach

In this first piece, the constant sound of the bass strings is intended to suggest the drone of a French bagpipe, or *musette.* This instrument was very popular in aristocratic circles—particularly the court of Louis XIV—in the late seventeenth and early eighteenth centuries.

To make sure that the alternating bass is kept up, and the drone sounded continuously throughout the piece, use a full barre across the second fret in measures thirteen through sixteen.

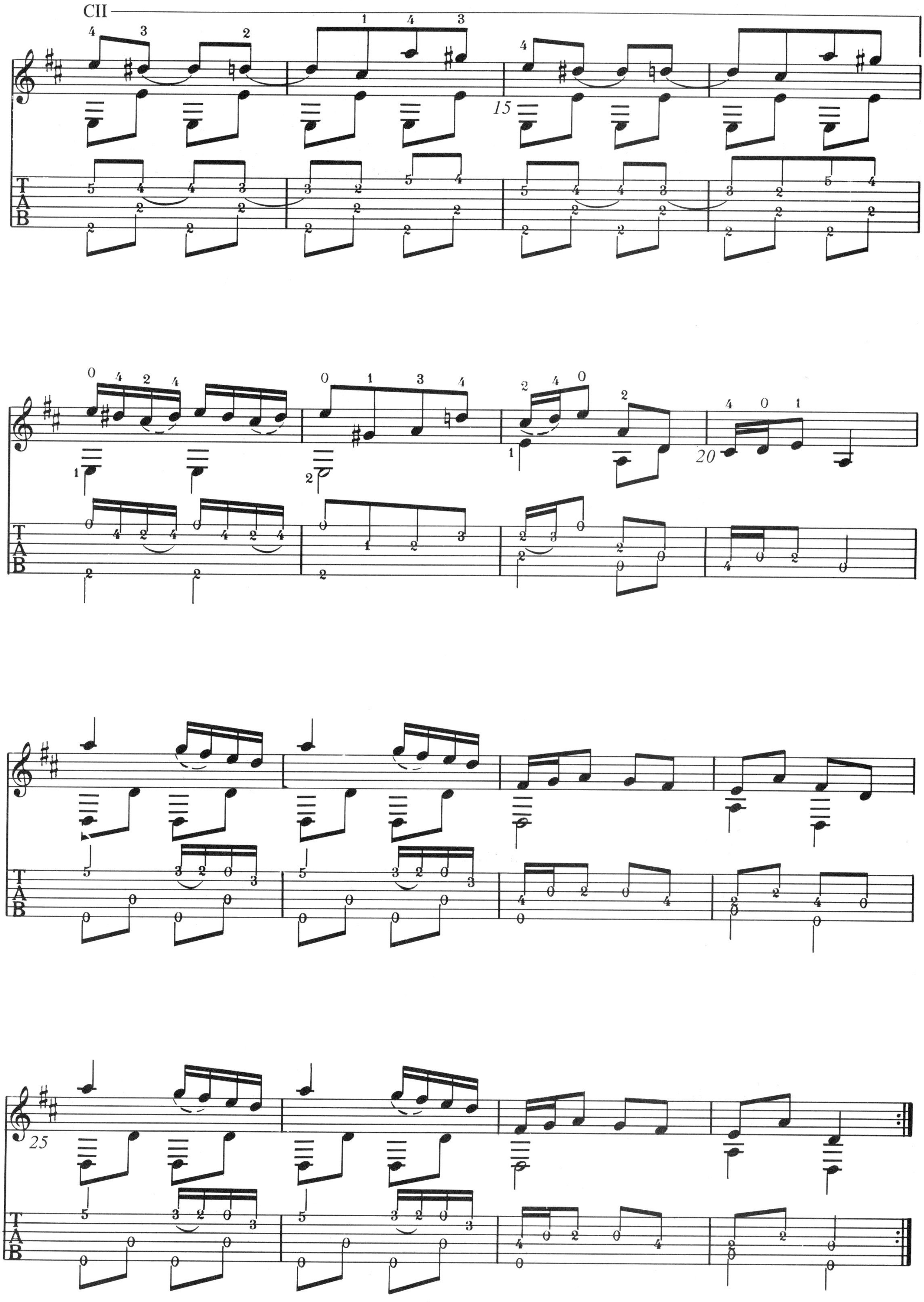
CII
15
20
25
TAB

Theme
from the Brandenburg Concerto No. 2 in F Major (*first movement*)

The Brandenburg Concertos are a set of six *concerti grossi* for various combinations of instruments commissioned by the Margrave of Brandenburg in 1721. At the time, this particular one was scored for flute, oboe, trumpet, and violin.

A barre used on the final beat in the third measure is an efficient way of fingering that particular phrase and allows the piece to continue in a strong, marchlike manner.

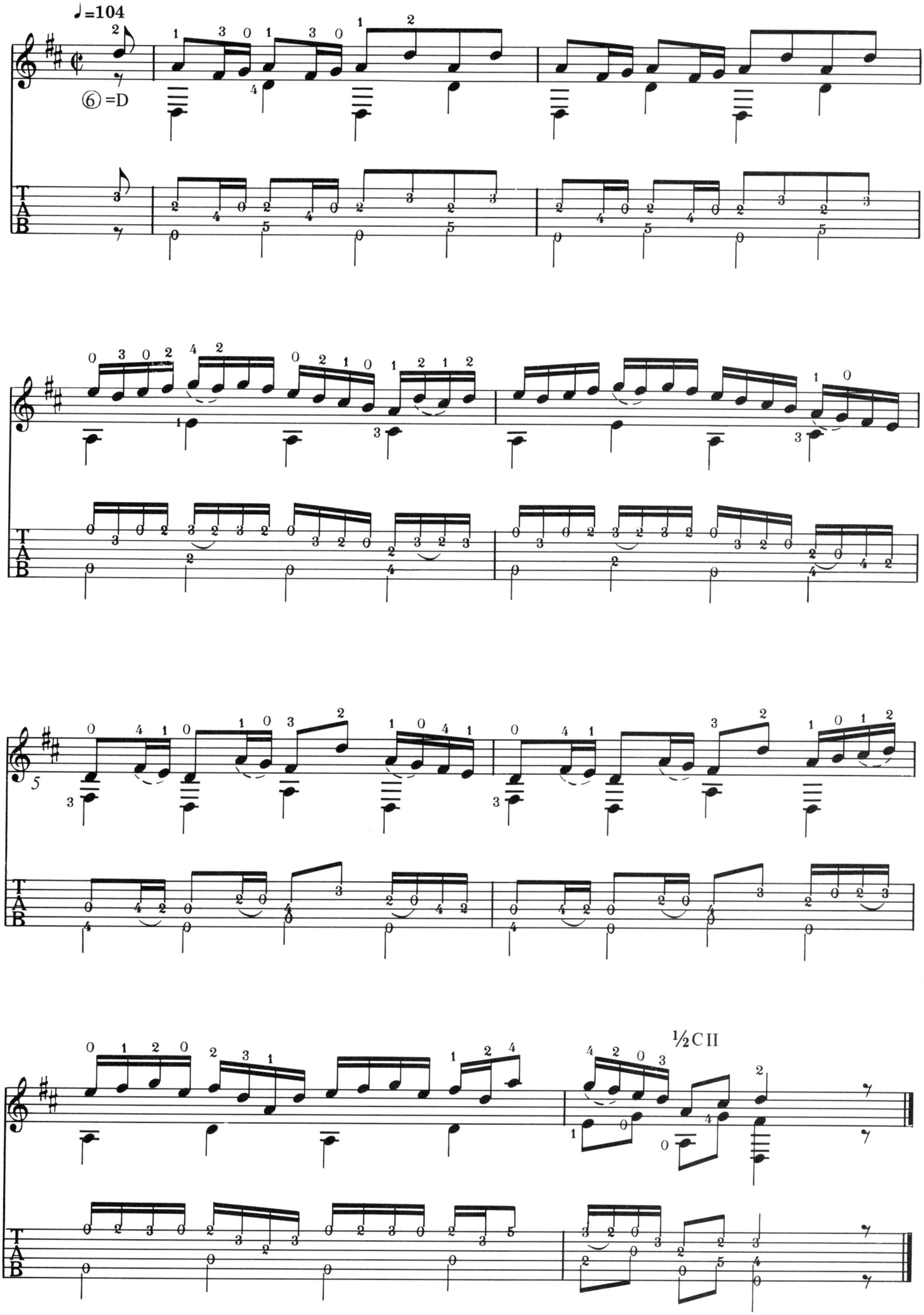
♩=104
⑥ =D
½ C II

Minuet

from the Notenbuch vor Anna Magdalena Bach

    The minuet was originally a rustic peasant dance that became so popular among the aristocracy that it was adopted as the official court dance in France during the latter half of the seventeenth century.

    This little minuet is from the *Notenbuch* (notebook) of Anna Magdalena Bach; a collection of simple but lovely instructional keyboard pieces written by Johann Sebastian for his second wife. The bass line in the B part has been altered slightly from the original in order to enhance the harmonic movment and give it the feel of a walking bass.

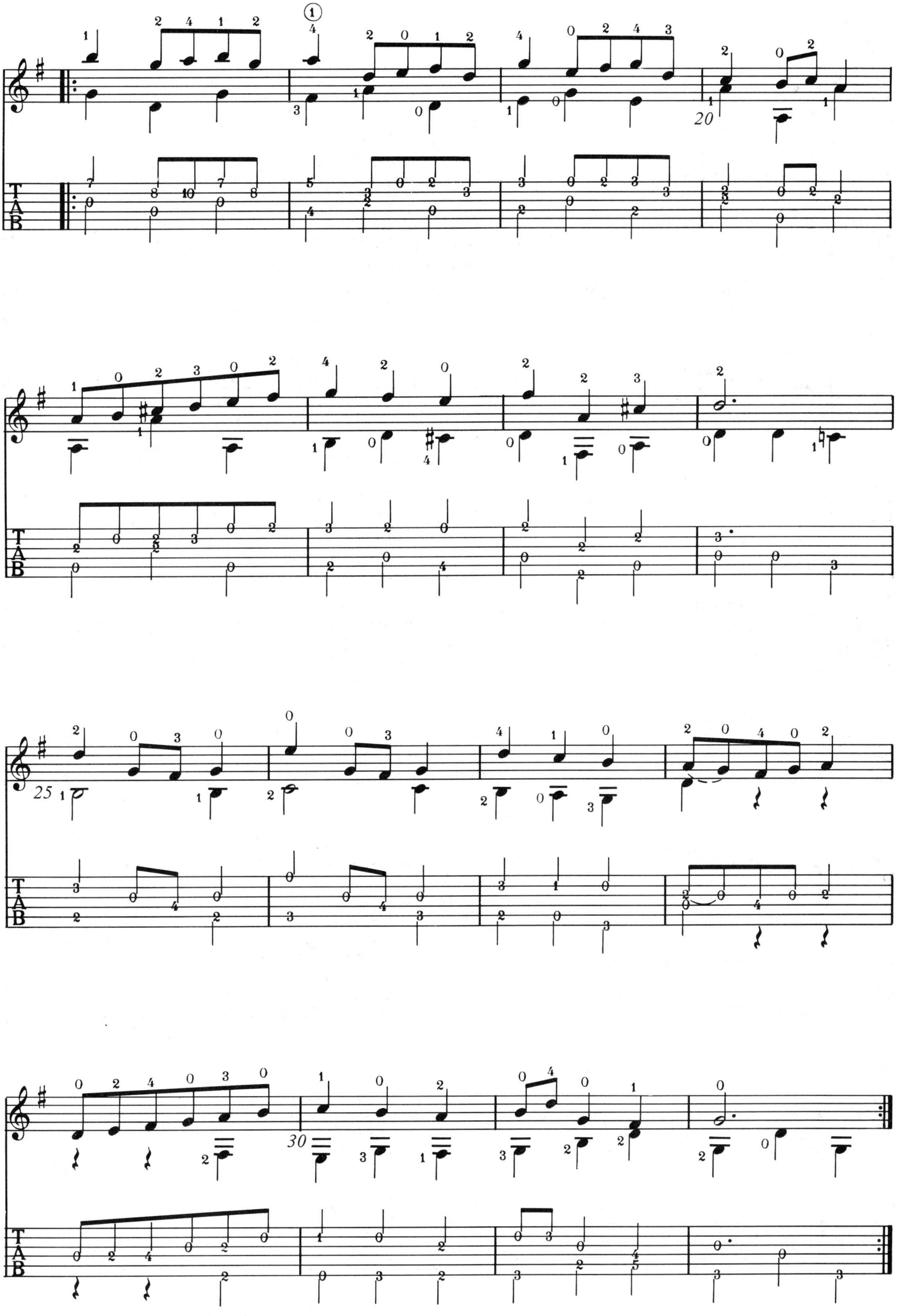
20
25
30

March

from the Notenbuch vor Anna Magdalena Bach

During the Baroque, the literature for harpsichord and lute were often interchangeable. As a result, this march required very little alteration from the original keyboard music, and should be played in a simple, gallant style.

For those who are learning these pieces mostly from the tablature, using barres in the first two measures will get the tempo off to a good, strong start. The Roman numerals preceded by a **C** (short for *capo*) in the music indicate exactly what frets are to be barred. In fact, if you are having difficulties coming up with a suitable fingering of your own, or if you'd like to speed up the learning process a bit, try going through and writing the fingering given with the music into the tablature. Also, thinking of the second half of the fourth measure as a C7 chord-form moved up two frets (making it a D7), might help to get the music "in your fingers," so to speak.

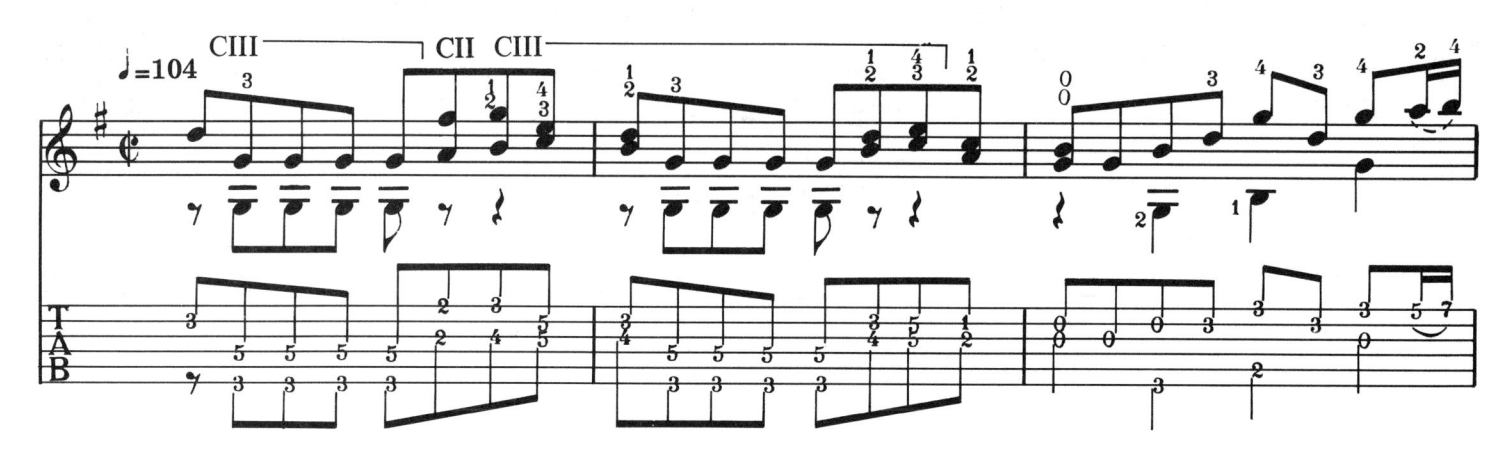

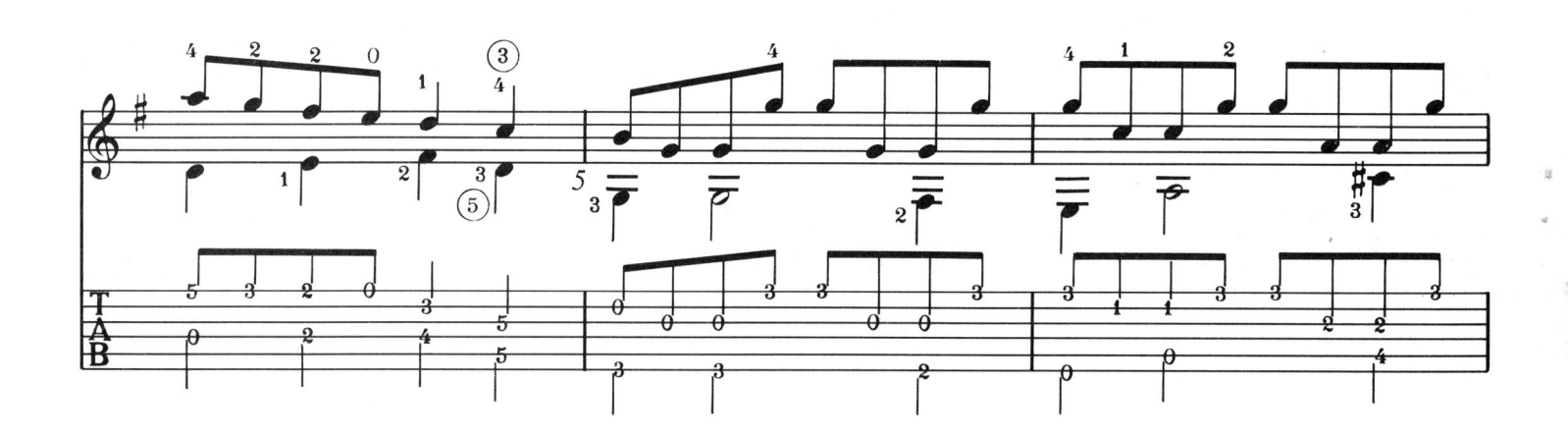

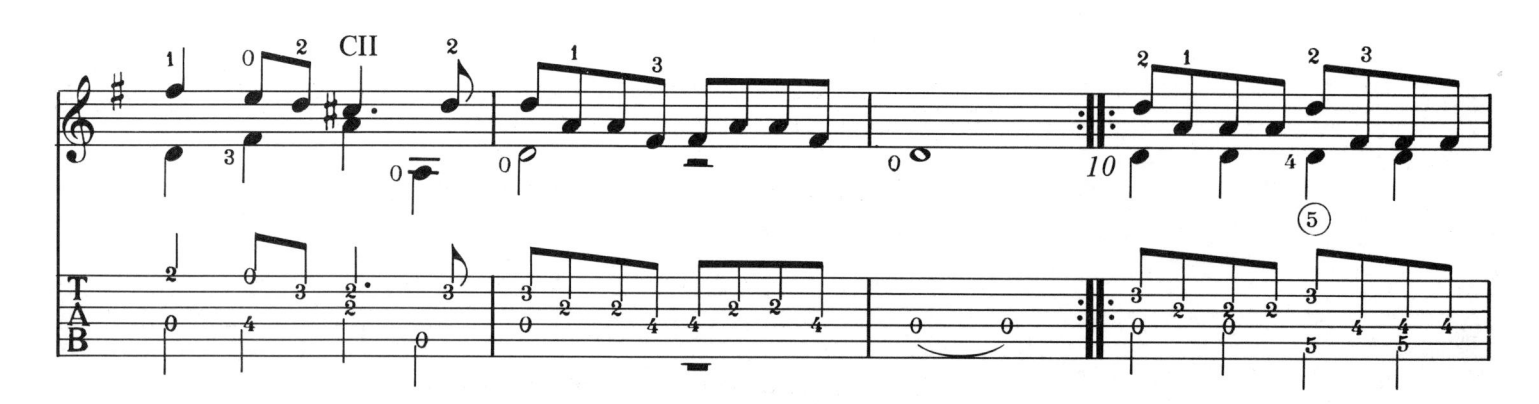

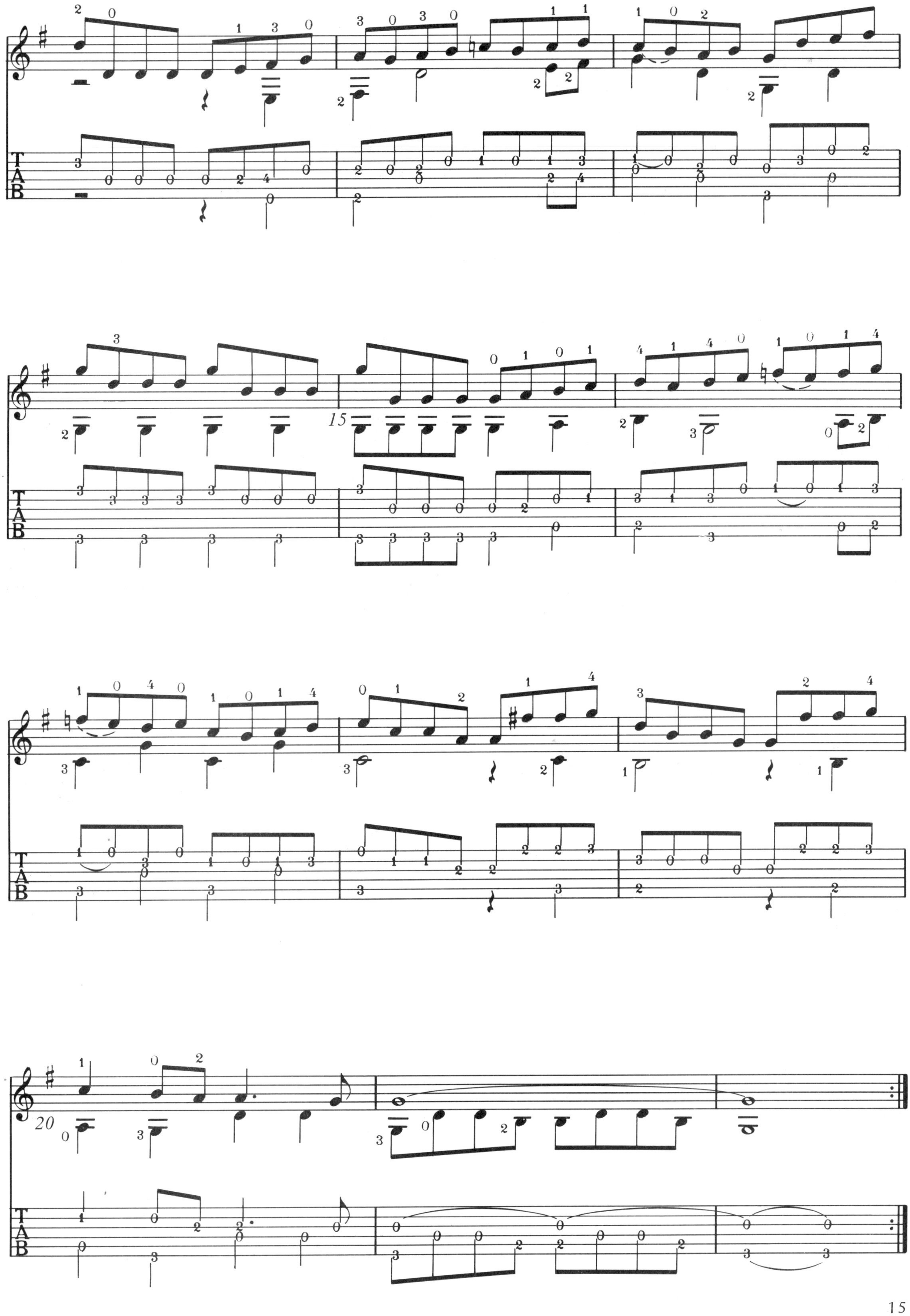

Jesu, Joy of Man's Desiring

Jesu bleibet meine Freude *from Cantata No. 147*

What is probably one of Bach's most famous compositions, *Jesu bleibet meine Freude* was written for Cantata No. 147 and scored for chorus, strings, and continuo. However, its beauty is so simple and transcendant, that arrangements have appeared for a variety of instruments and ensembles as disparate in tone and tradition as church organ, 5-string banjo, and rock-n-roll band ("Joy" by Apollo 100).

It's possible to personalize this particular arrangement, and give it more of a fingerpicking feel, by inserting more hammer-ons and pull-offs throughout.

Measures four, twelve, and thirteen will probably go easier for you if the second finger (sounding an A) is held down throughout.

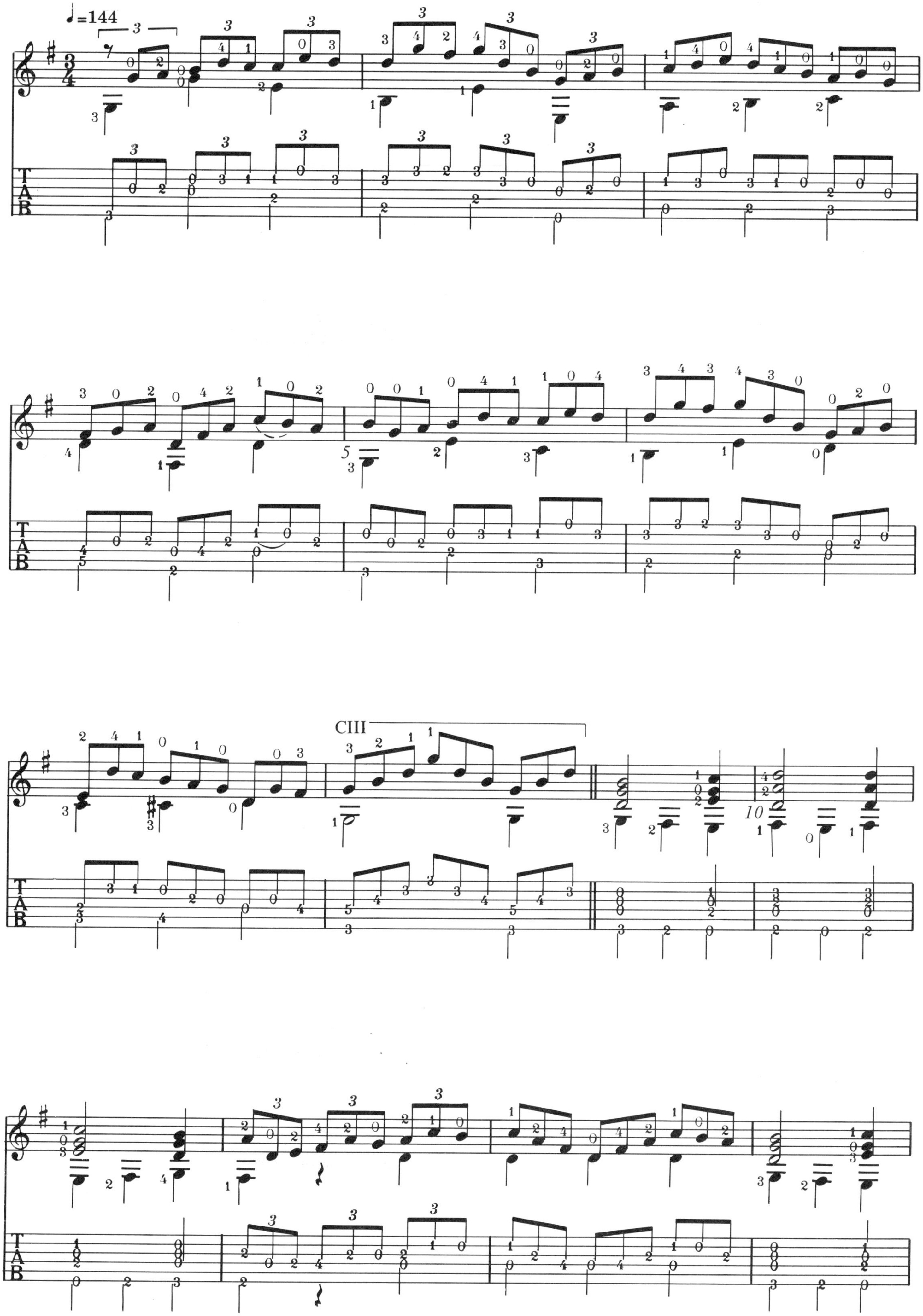
♩=144
CIII

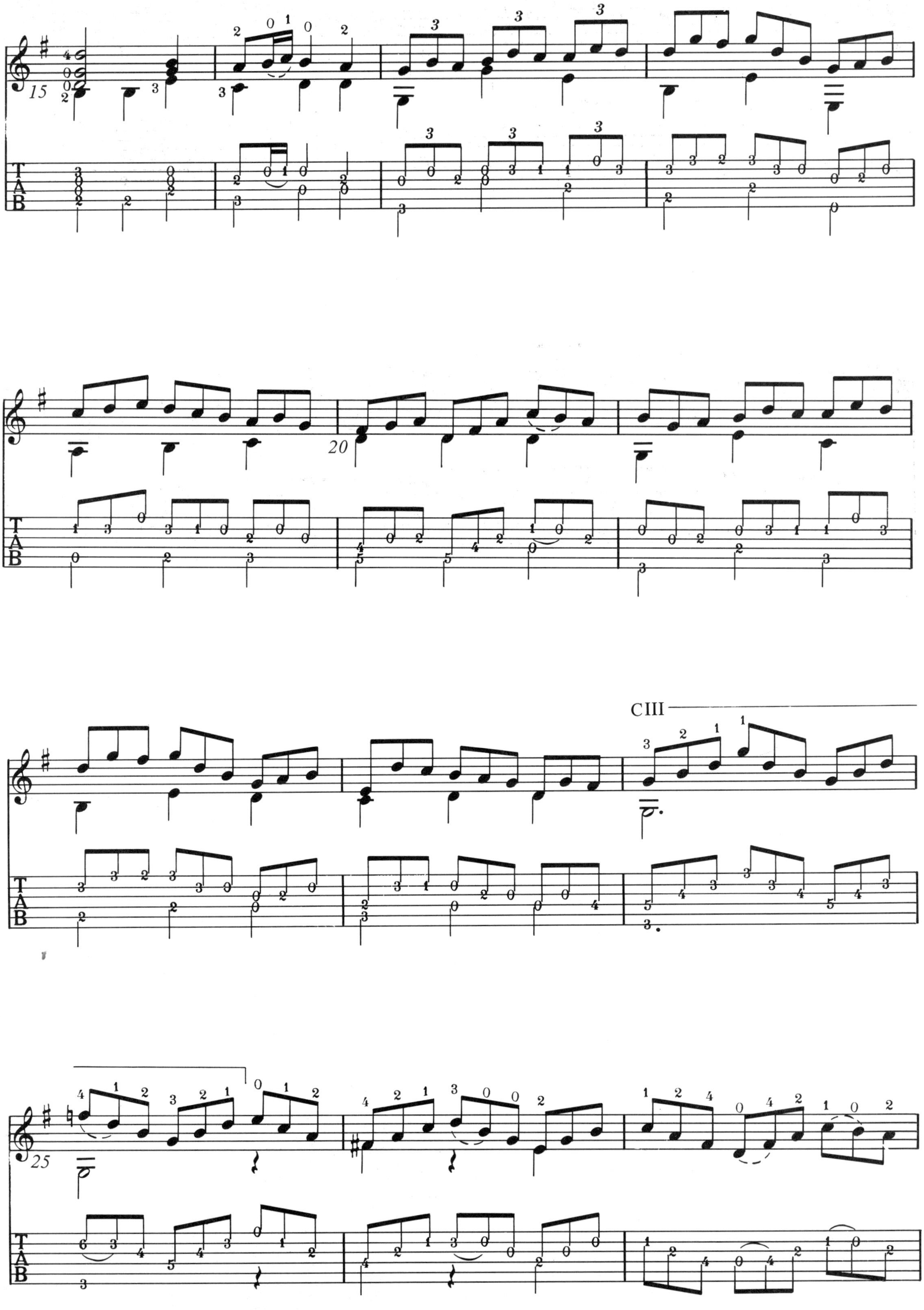
CIII

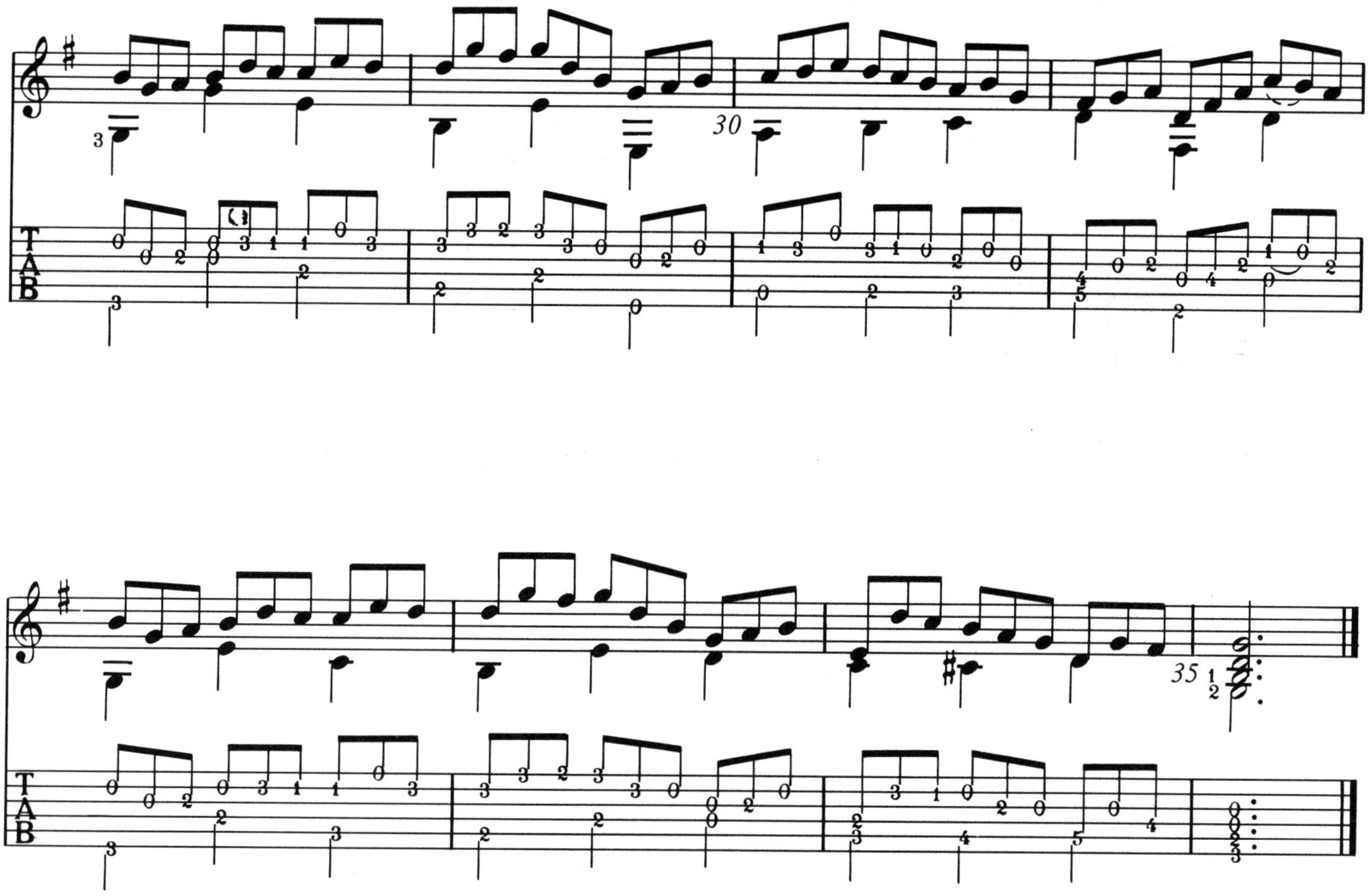
30
35

Gavotte I and II
from the sixth Cello Suite

The gavotte is a lively dance written in *Da Capo* form (A A B B C C D D A B) and is usually characterized by phrases that begin and end in the middle of a measure. It is possible that its name is derived from the *Gavots*; inhabitants of the Pays de Gaps in France. The two pieces here should be played lightly, in a style similar to that of the musette. In measures two, five, and twenty-one, the pull-offs to the C can be performed more simply by holding down the low F and barring across the first fret. The same technique, while a bit more complicated, can also be used in measure twenty-five. The F♯ in measure seven is played twice, so keep that second finger down.

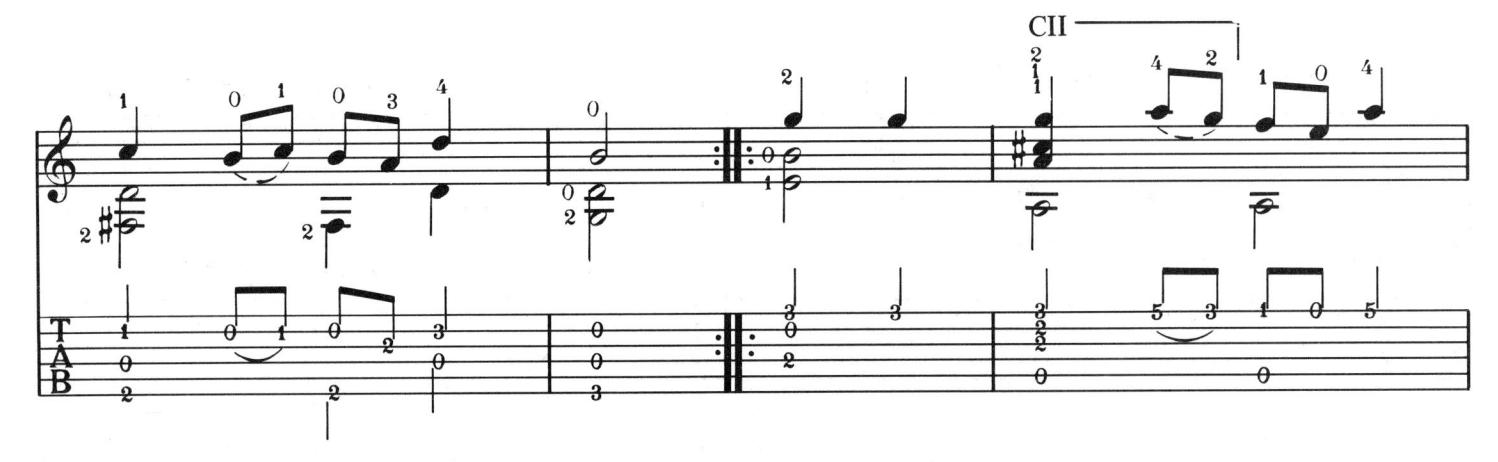

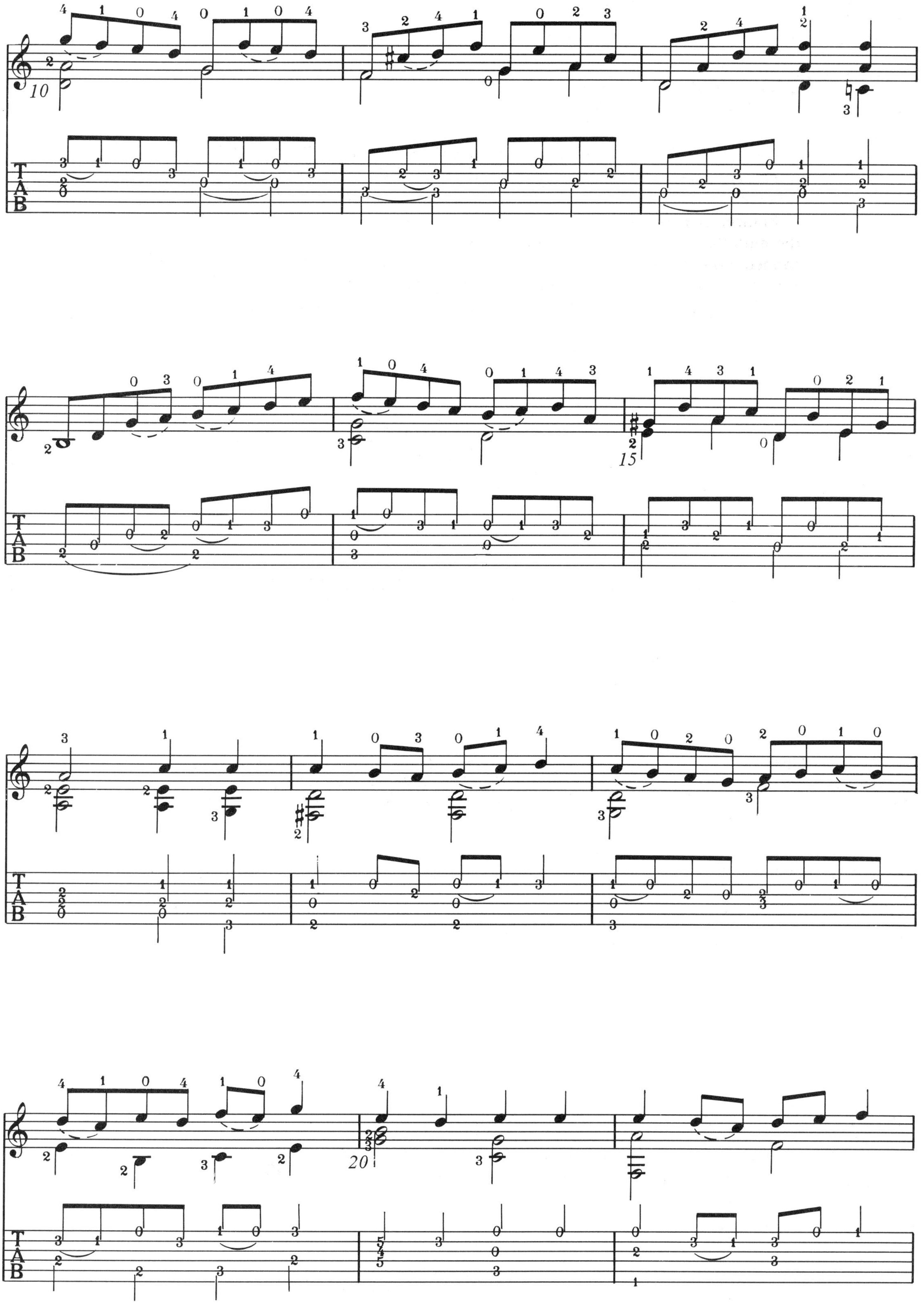
10
15
20

Gavotte II

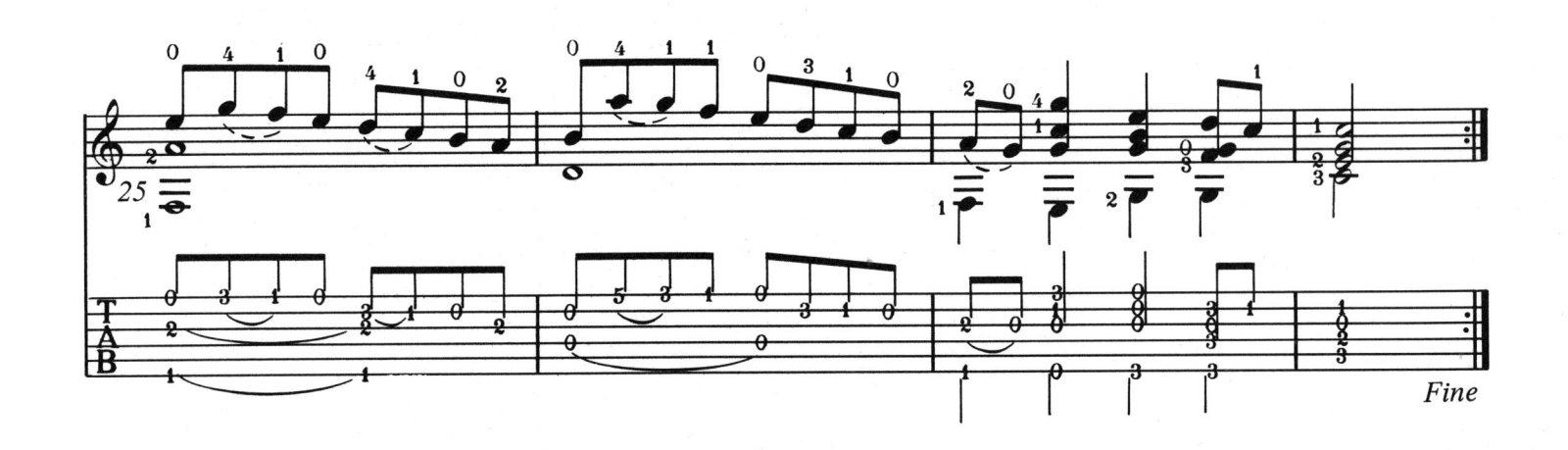

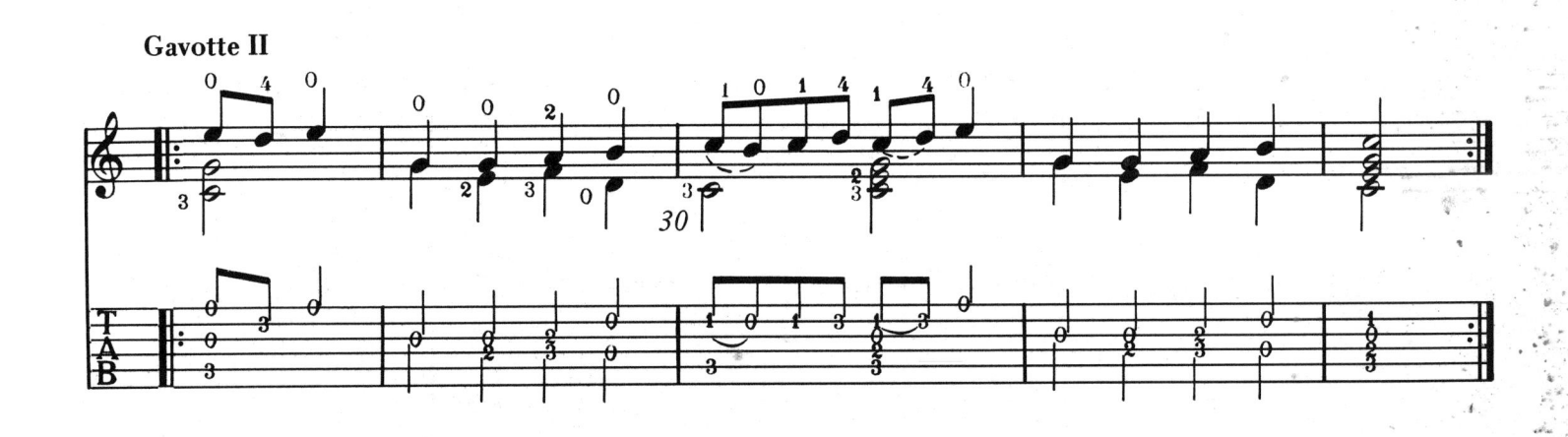

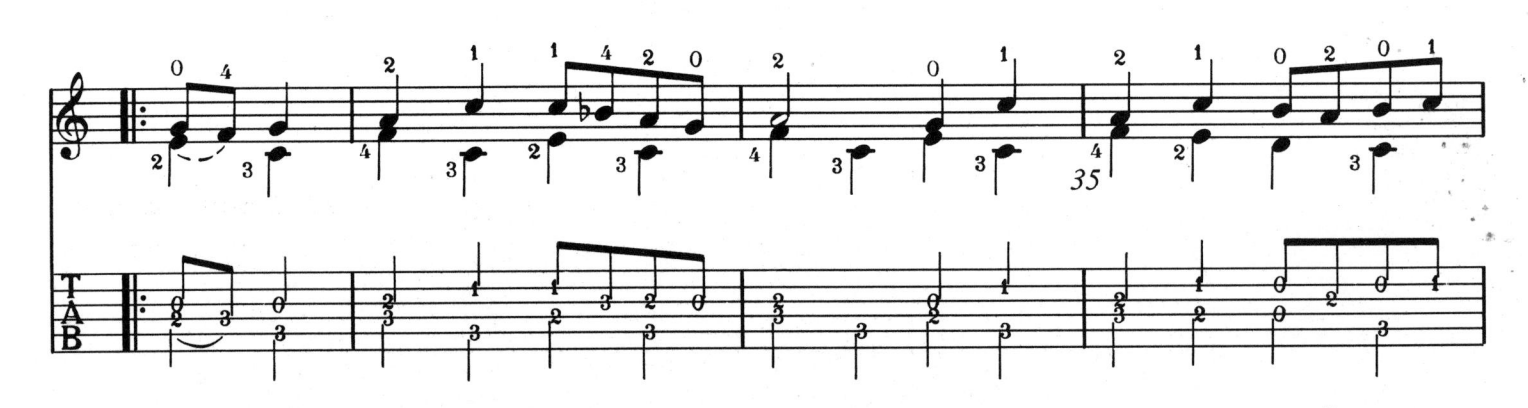

D.C. Gavotte I al Fine

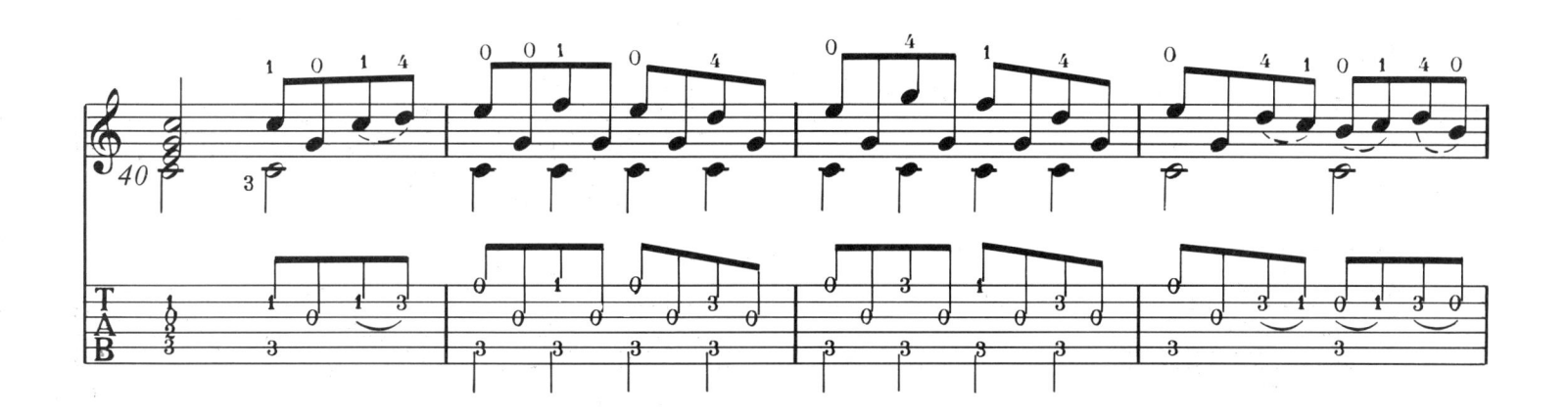

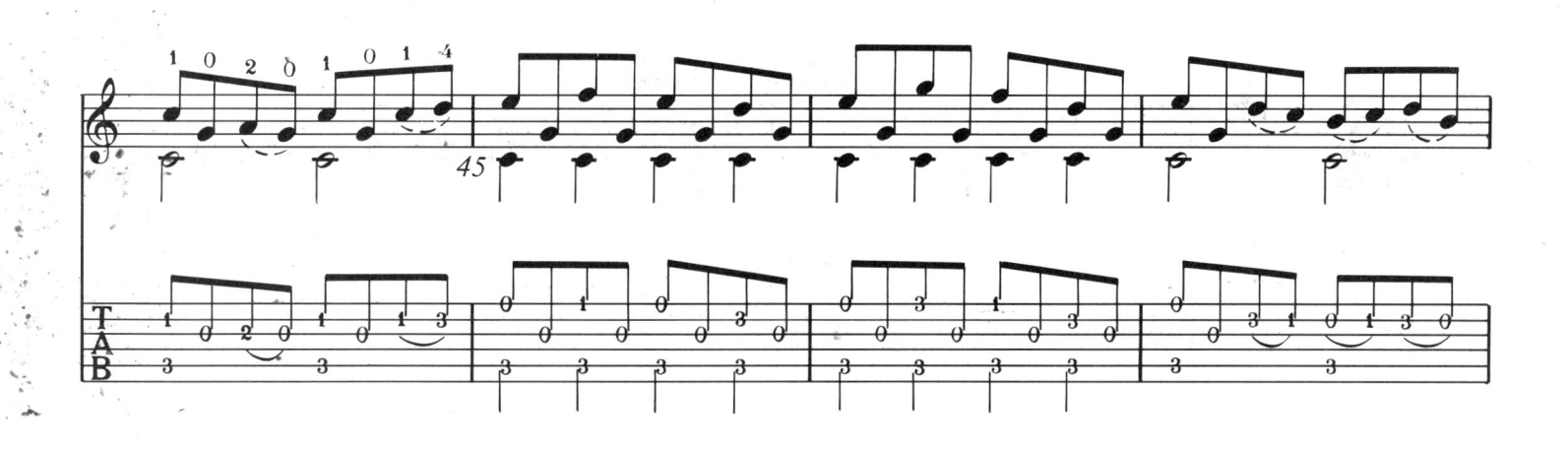

Sleepers Awake!

Wachet Auf *from Cantata No. 140*

It would be unfortunate to allow the slow, stately dignity of this piece to remind one only of the tedium of an endless graduation processional. It is taken from Cantata No. 140, written for the twenty-seventh Sunday after Trinity, and is actually a countermelody used as a setting for a hymn-tune by Philipp Nicolai which continues to be used in current hymnals and church services.

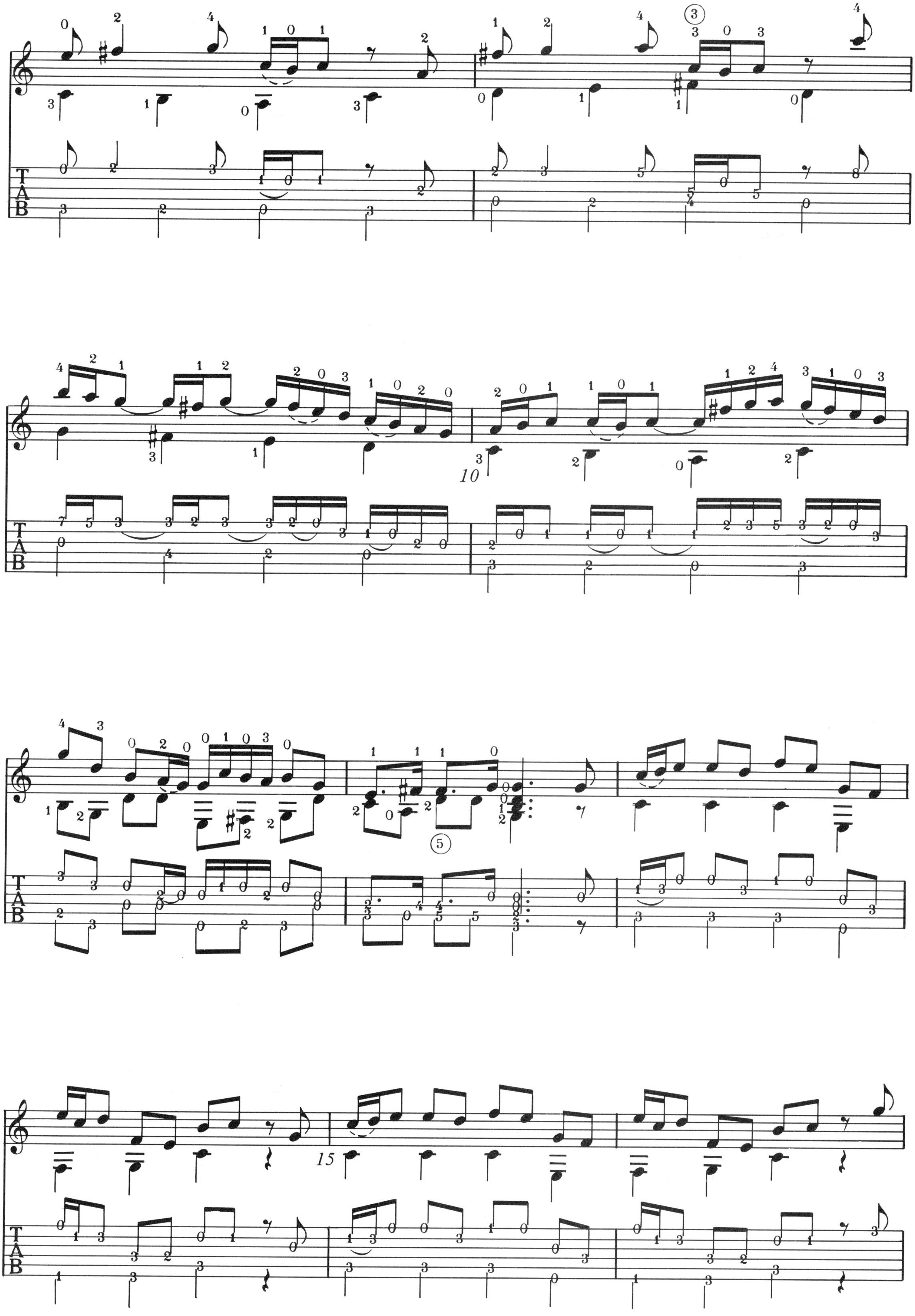

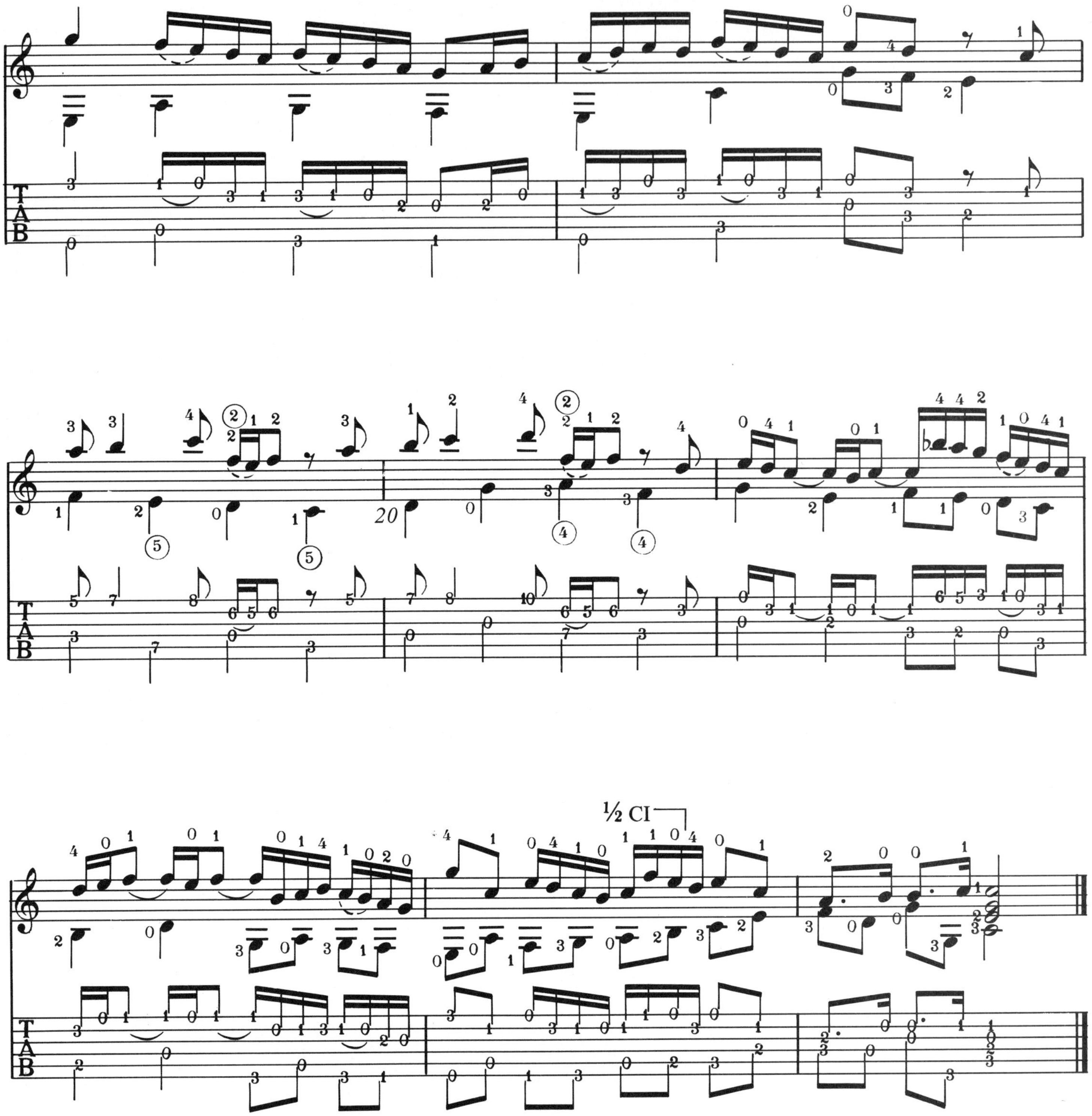
½ CI

O Sacred Head Now Wounded
O Haupt voll Blut und Wunden *from the* Passion according to Saint Matthew

Many of you will identify this immediately as "American Tune" by Paul Simon. Originally it was used as a recurring melodic theme in the *Saint Matthew Passion*.

Before reading straight through this one, it might help to go through and find as many traditional chord-forms as possible. For example, the notes in the third and fourth beats of measure three outline a B7 chord; and thinking of measure five as a D7 changing to a C and then back to a D7 will help get it in your fingers a lot faster.

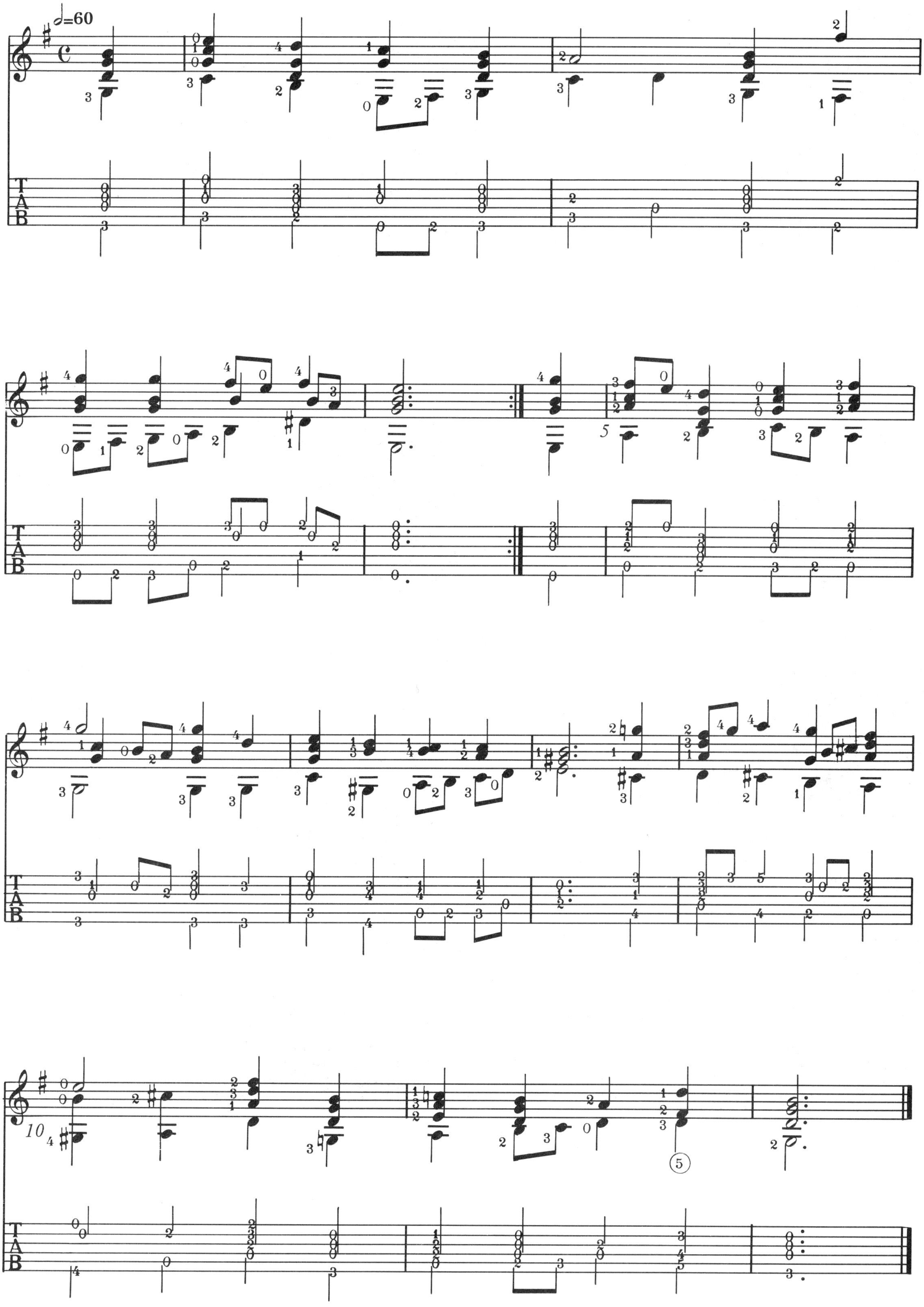
=60

Gavotte I and II
from the Orchestral Suite No. 3 in D Major

Bach wrote four Orchestral Suites, each with an overture followed by a series of pieces that are primarily dances. They were most likely written for the orchestra at Cöthen which Bach directed until his move to Leipzig in 1723.

Like the arrangement for "O Sacred Head Now Wounded," there are many easily recognizeable chord-forms in the first gavotte. For example, in the last two beats of measure seven there is a D7 chord played using a C7 chord-form moved up two frets. Thinking of a B7 moved up one fret will help in understanding the second half of measure twenty-two.

The second gavotte should be a bit more legato and laid-back than the first. If you hold your fingers down in measure thirty-three, you'll notice that most of that measure can be thought of as a D7 chord with an F♯ in the bass. Measures fifty-one and fifty-two will seem difficult at first, but work slowly and follow the fingering and it will come to you faster.

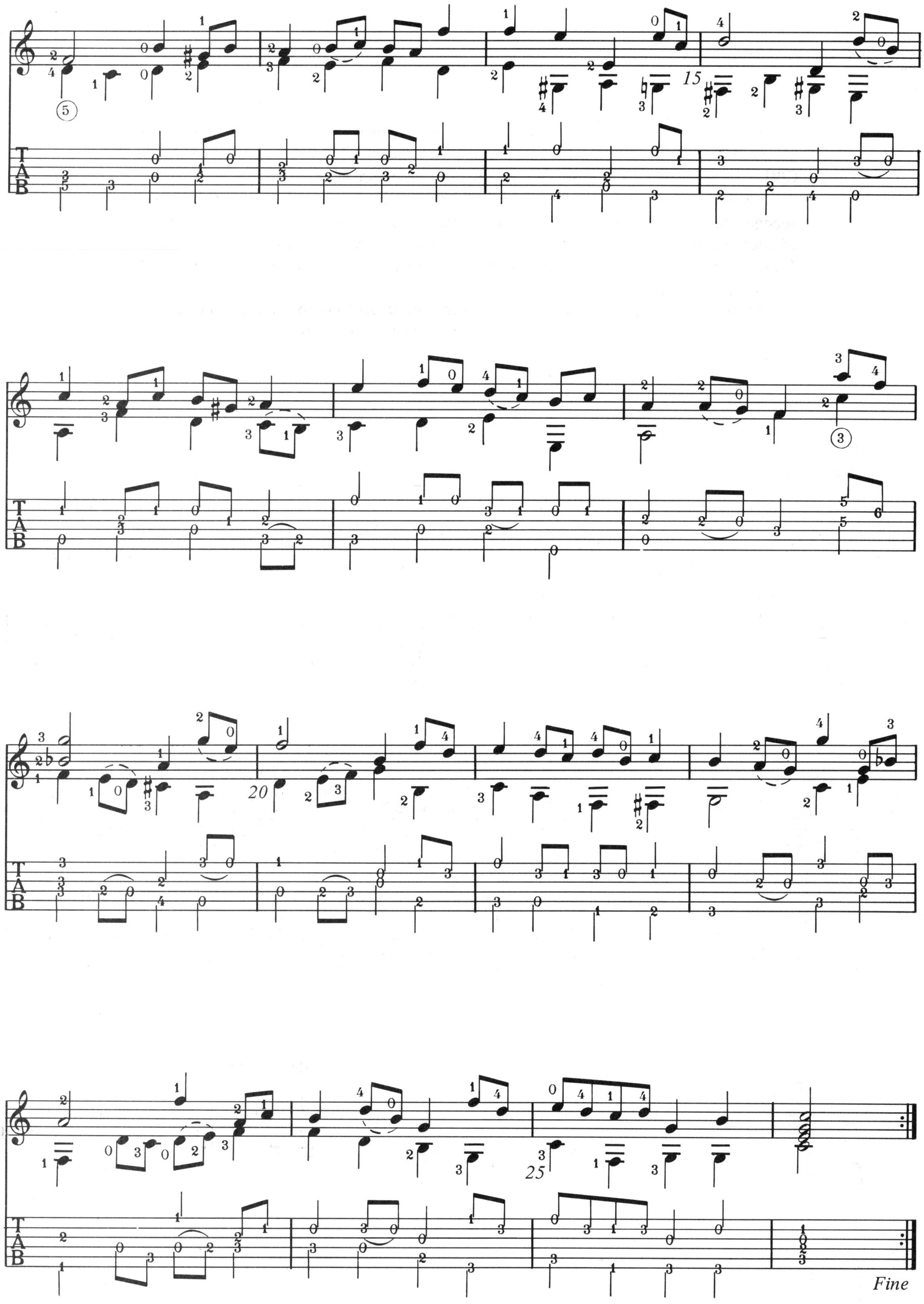
15
20
25
Fine

Gavotte II

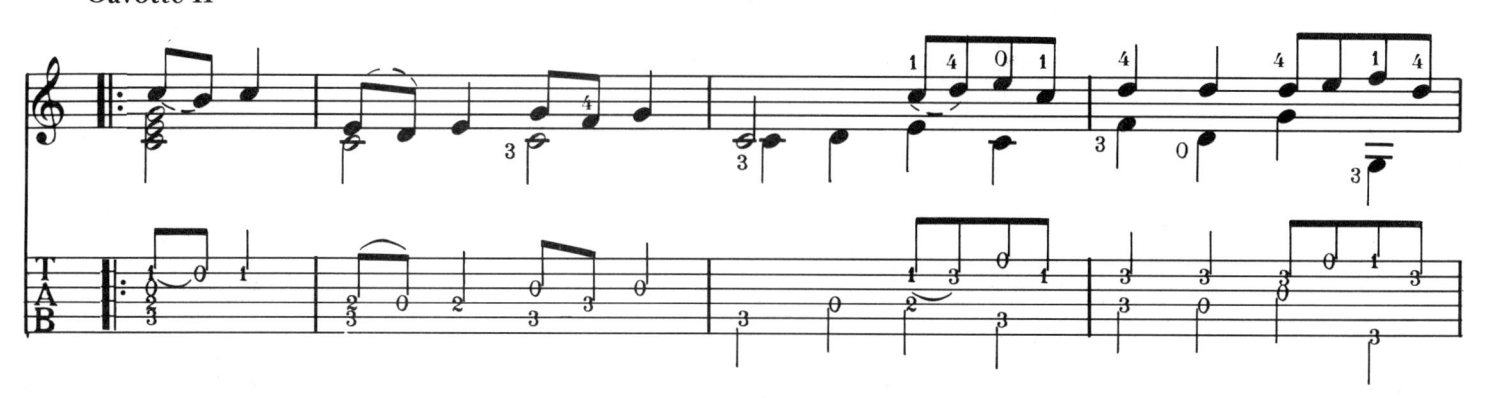

D.C. Gavotte I al Fine

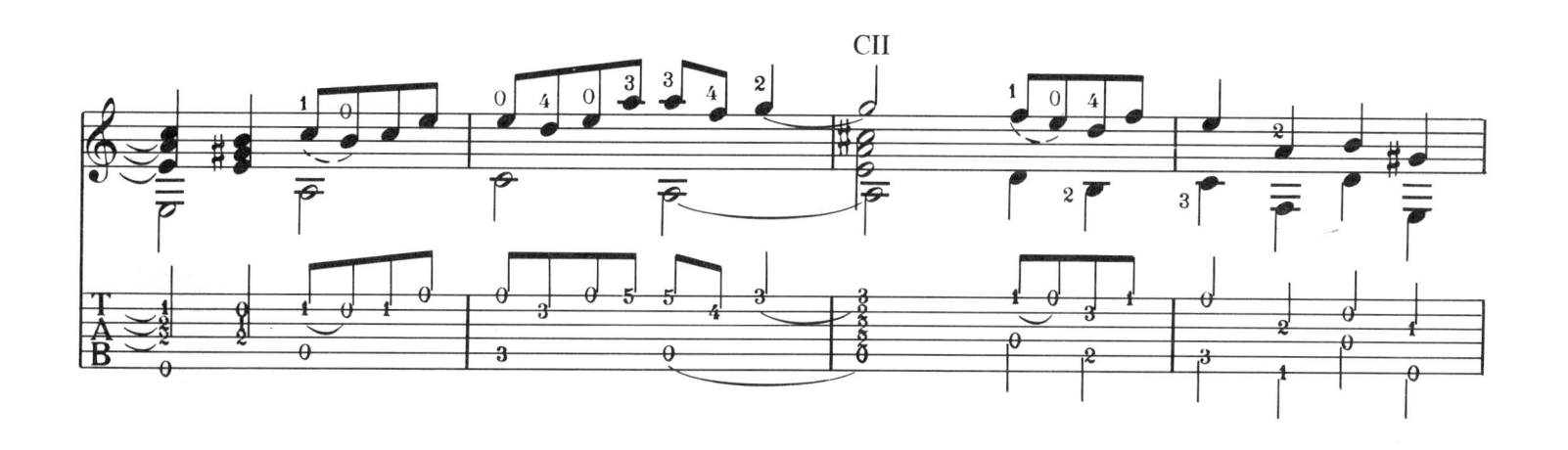

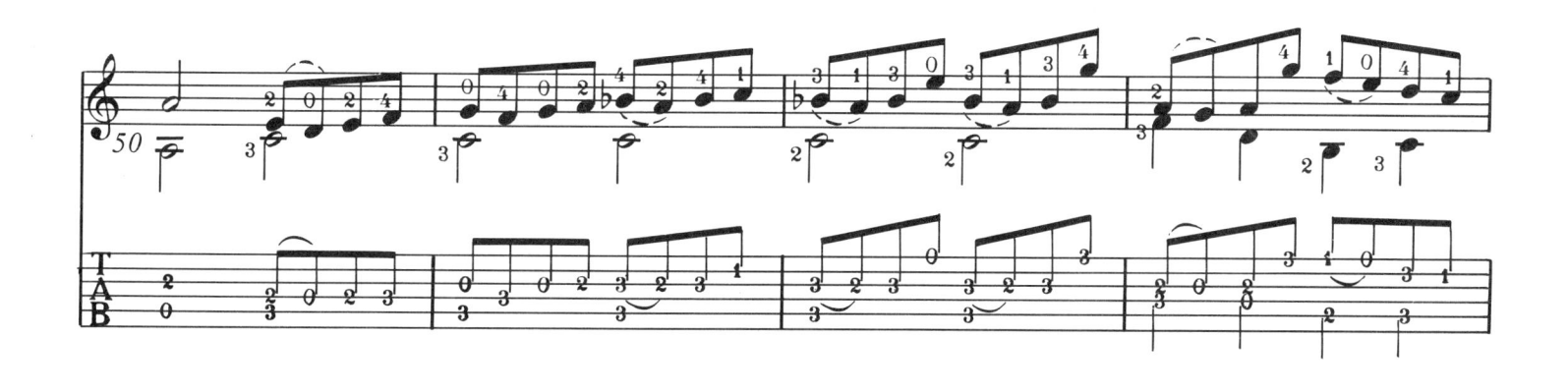

Bourree
from the first Lute Suite

Like the minuet, the bourree began as a French peasant dance. Bourrees traditionally employ phrasing that begins on the fourth beat of the measure, and so start with a single upbeat. They are generally executed in a joyful, quick, and even manner (as opposed to the swingy version popularized by Jethro Tull).

Although this piece may sound a bit more "note-y" than some of the other pieces in the book, it is still possible to comprehend most of the phrases as chord changes. Hold the second finger down in measure three (the A) all the way through to measure four. The bass line in measures twenty-one and twenty-two can be played very effectively by using a right-hand pattern of thumb-index-thumb (*p-i-p*) for each of the two three-note phrases.

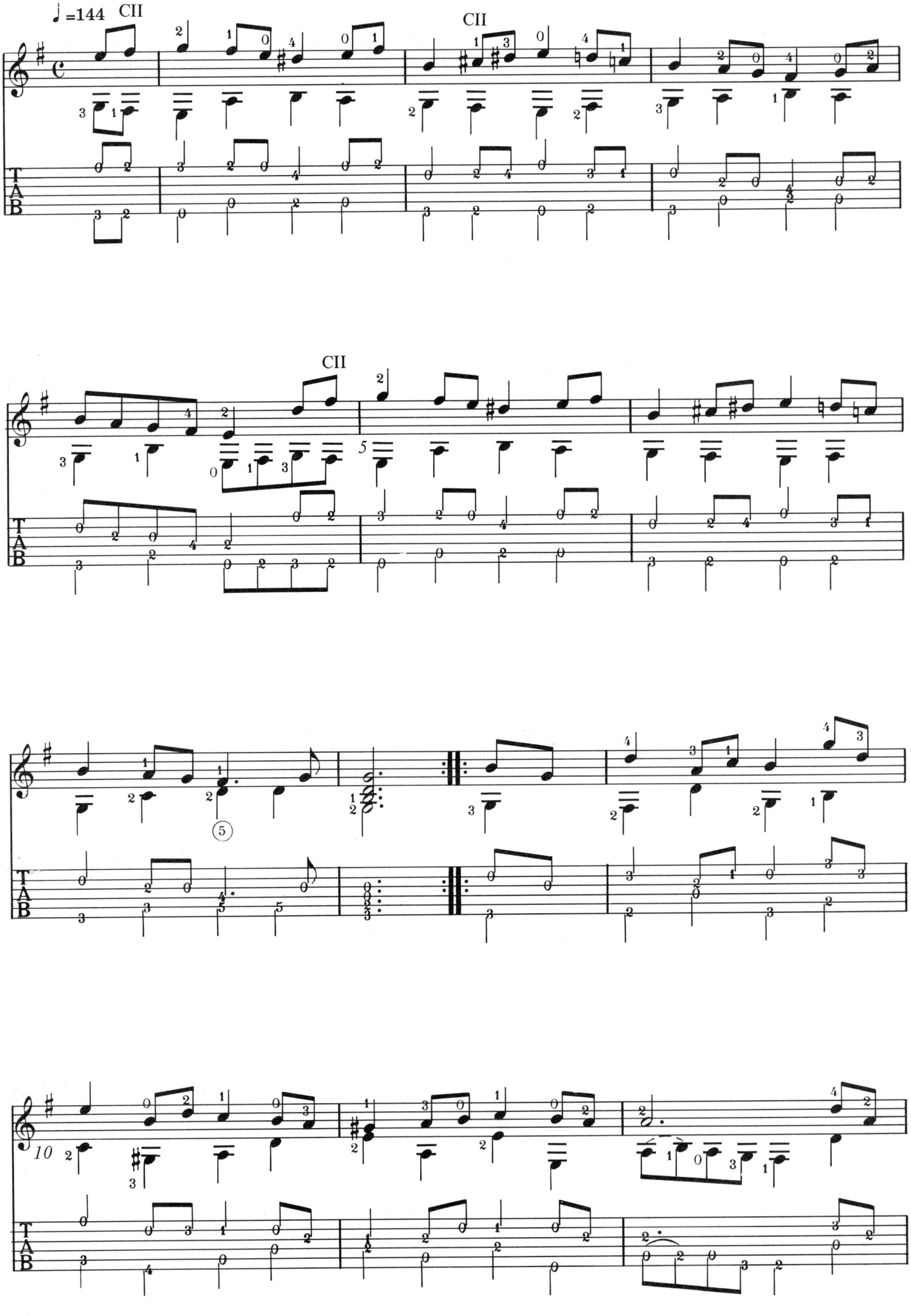
=144
CII
CII
CII

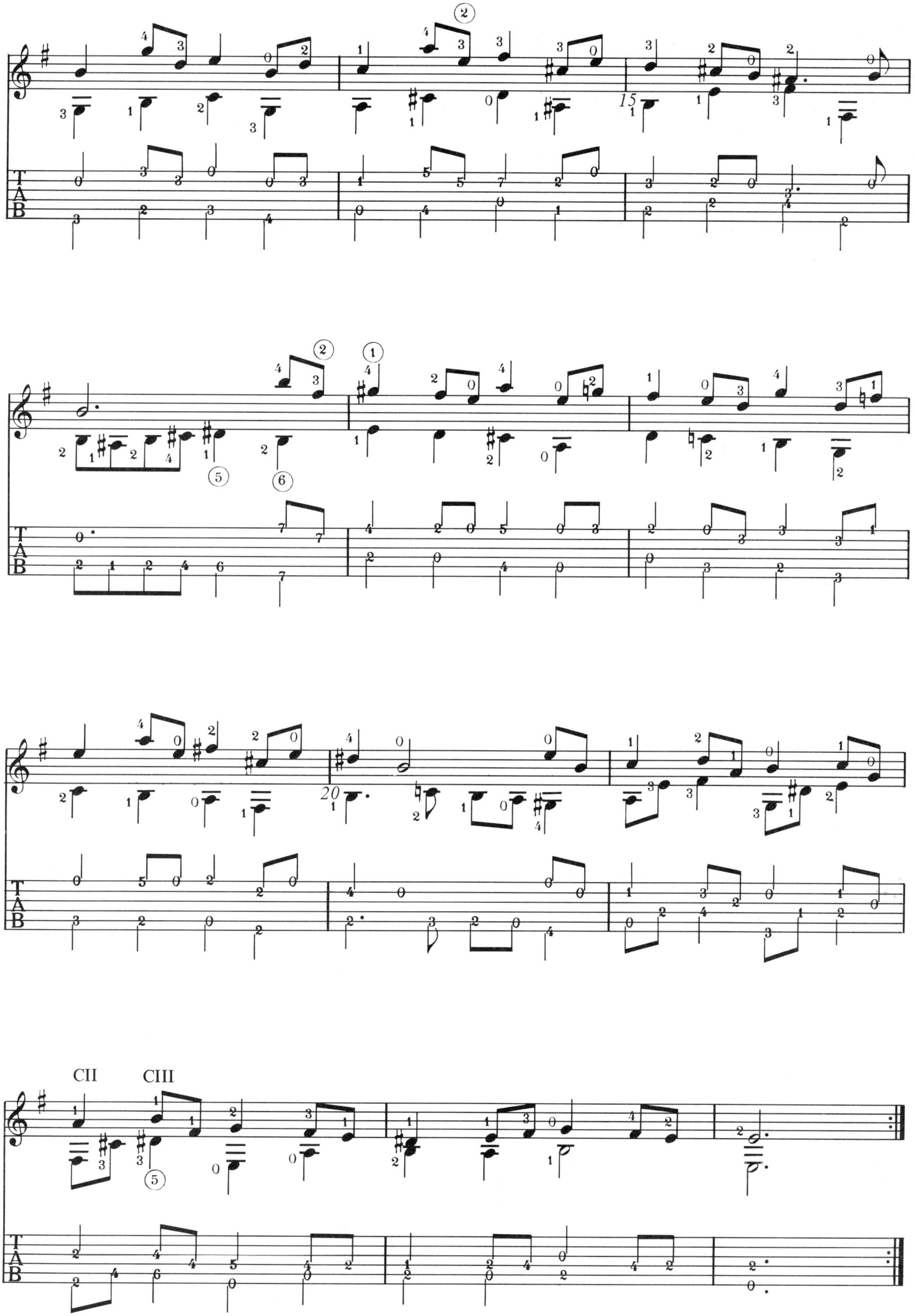
15
20
CII
CIII

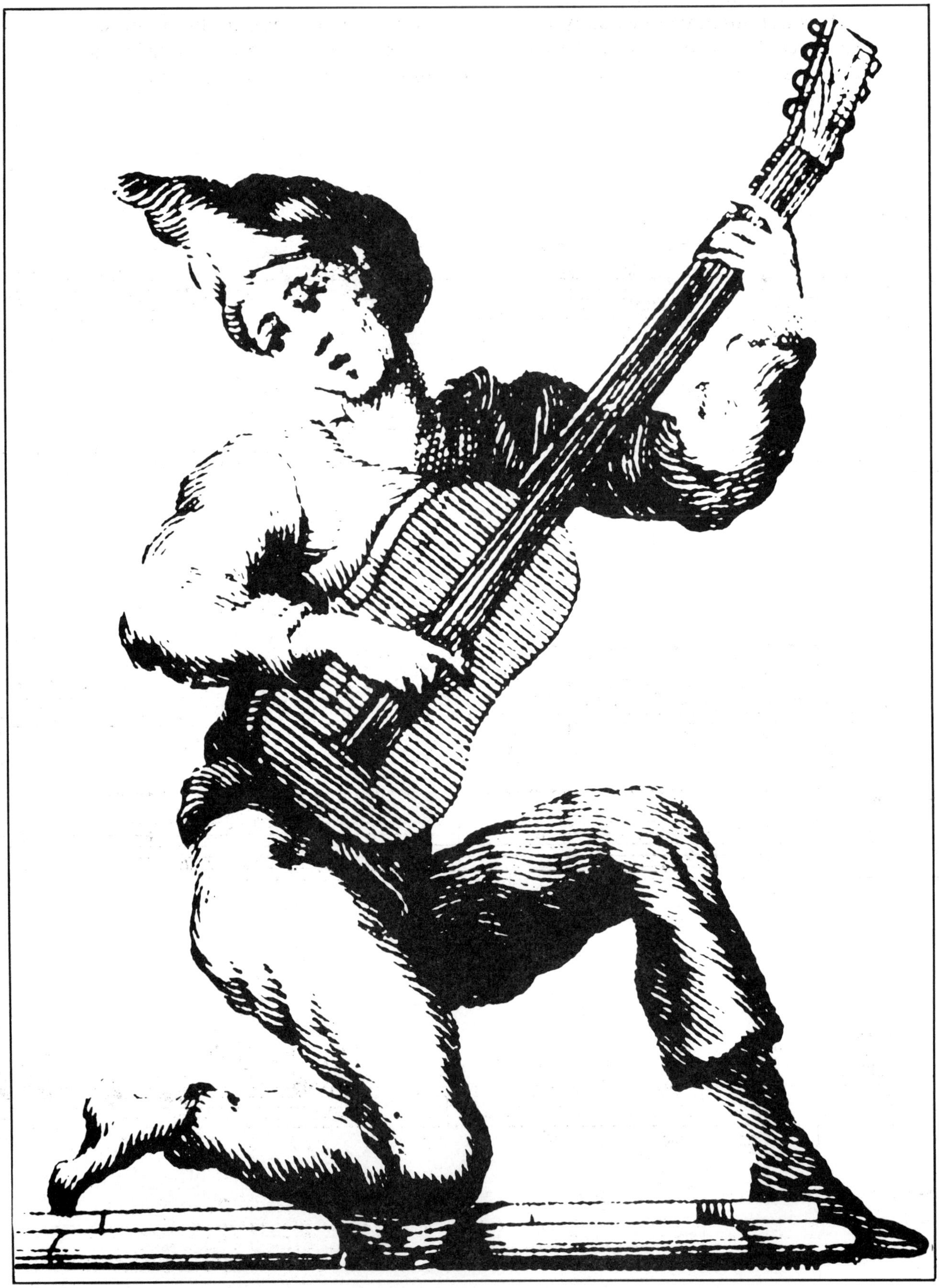

Gavotte
from the third Lute Suite

There are some surprisingly jazzlike harmonies to be found throughout this gavotte. It is from the third of the four Lute Suites which is actually Bach's own transcription of his fifth Cello Suite.

It is not absolutely necessary to hold the D♯ throughout measure twenty-seven. However, it would be helpful to hold the A through to measure twenty-eight and once again understand the last two beats of measure twenty-seven as a chord form.

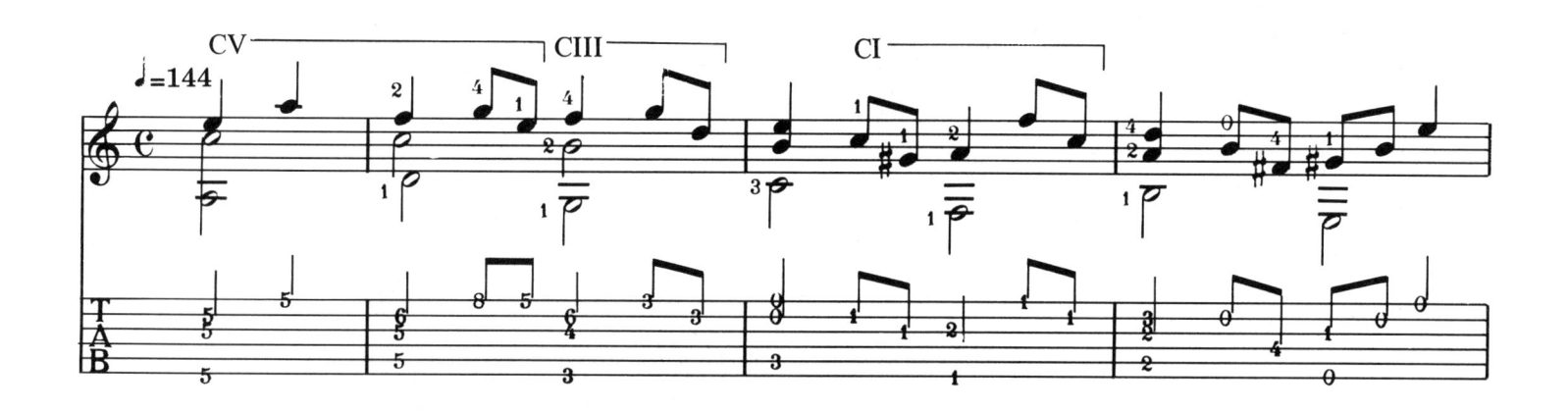

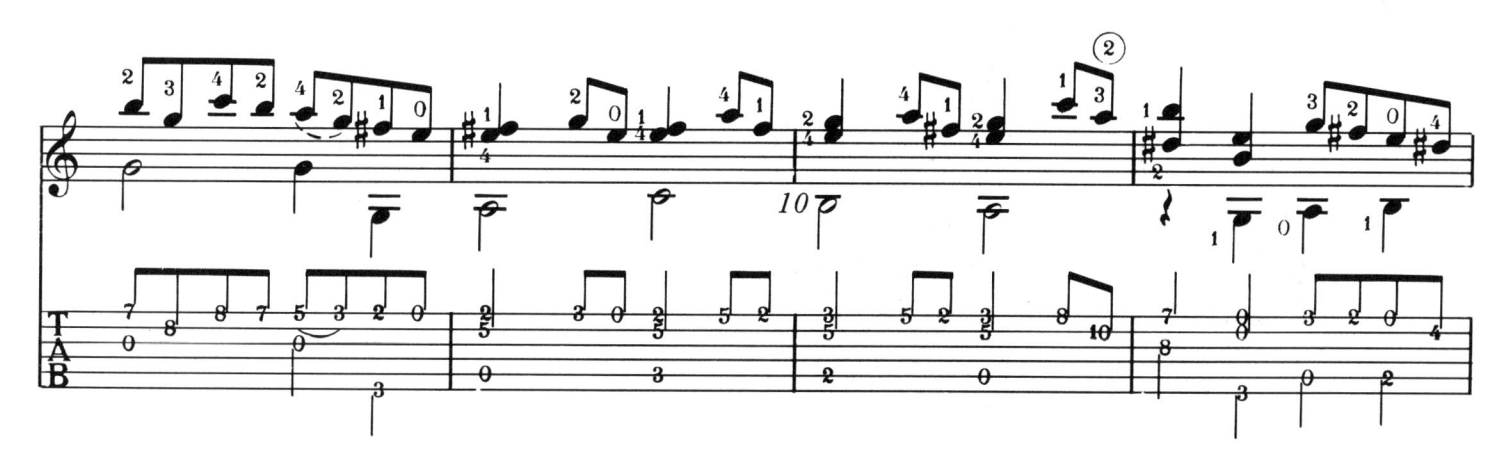

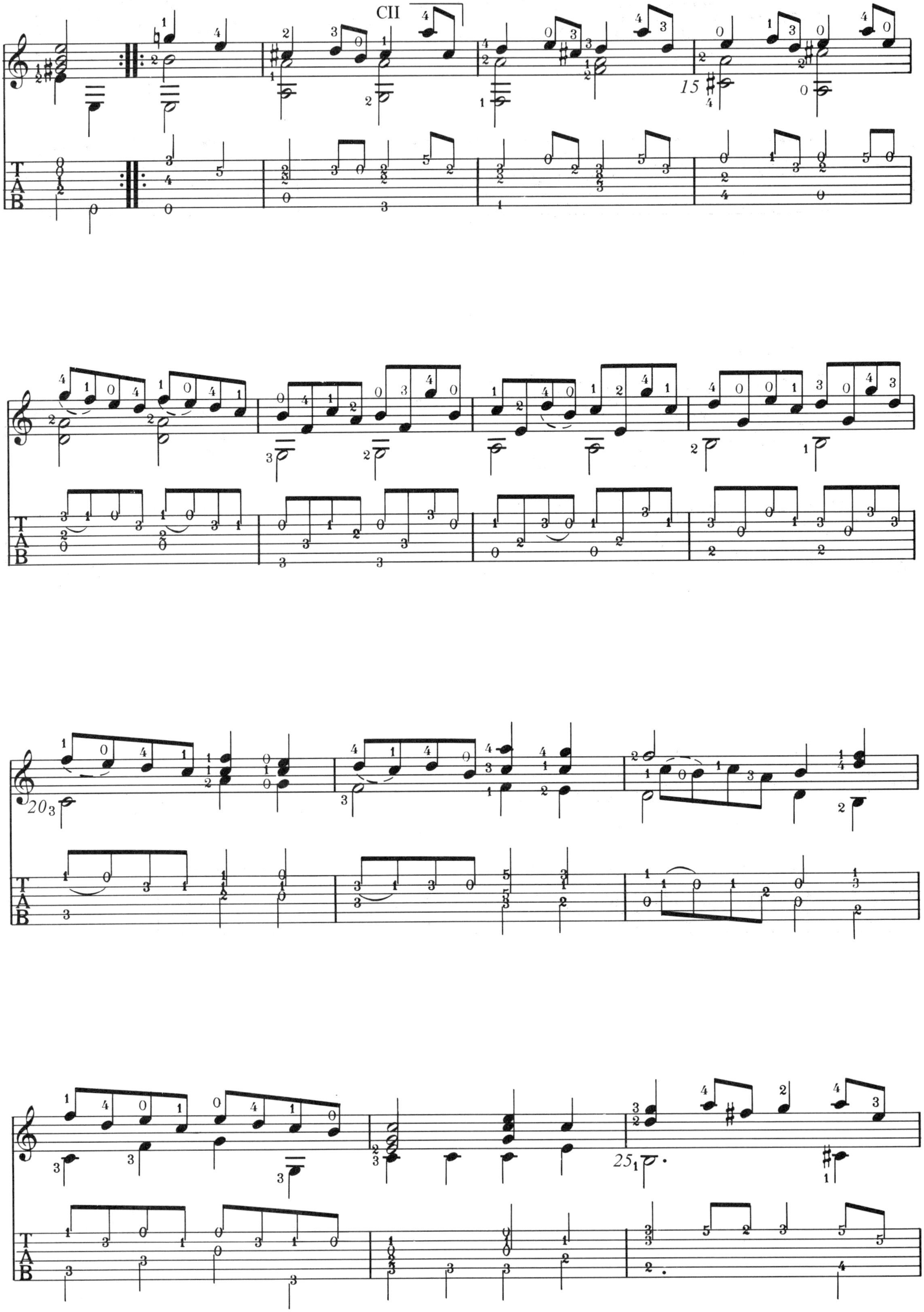
CII
15
20
25

41

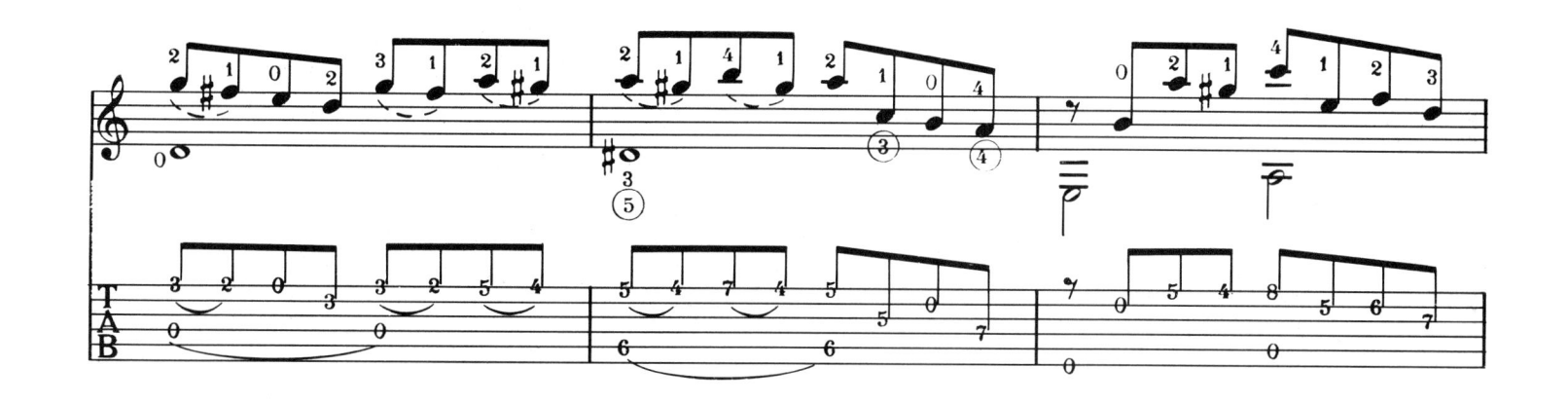

Badinerie
from the Orchestral Suite No. 2 in B Minor

Originating from a French word meaning alternately playfulness, banter, or teasing, this badinerie is from the *Orchestral Suite No. 2 in B Minor,* and is most famous as a bravura flute composition. It has been fingered with many open strings, in order to make it flow. You'll find that hammer-ons, pull-offs, and other fingerpicking techniques adapt nicely to its overall sound.

If the extreme shifts up and down the neck seem a bit intimidating, try working them out as chords. For example, the very first measure is simply a D-minor chord-form played on the eighth fret.

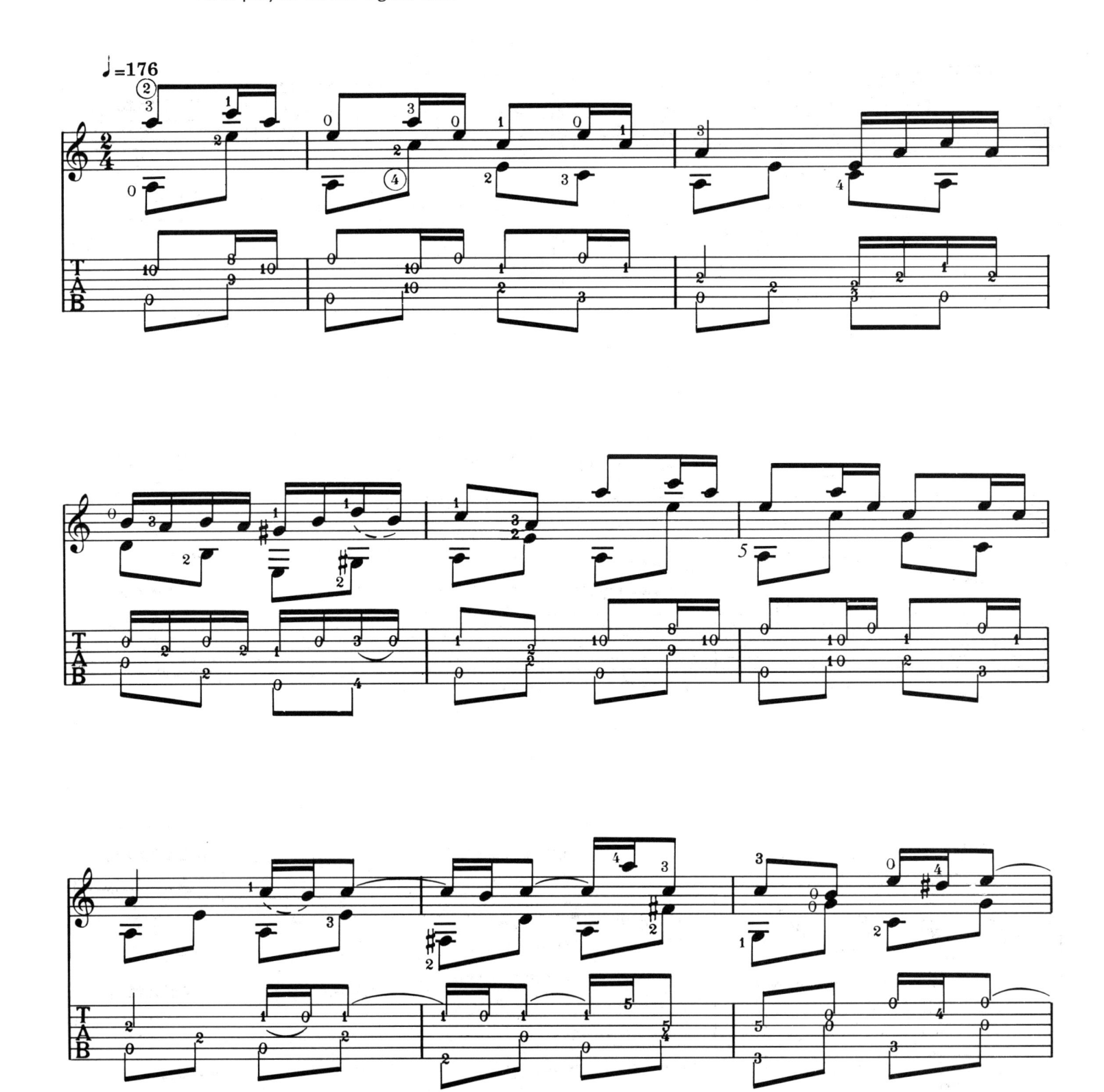

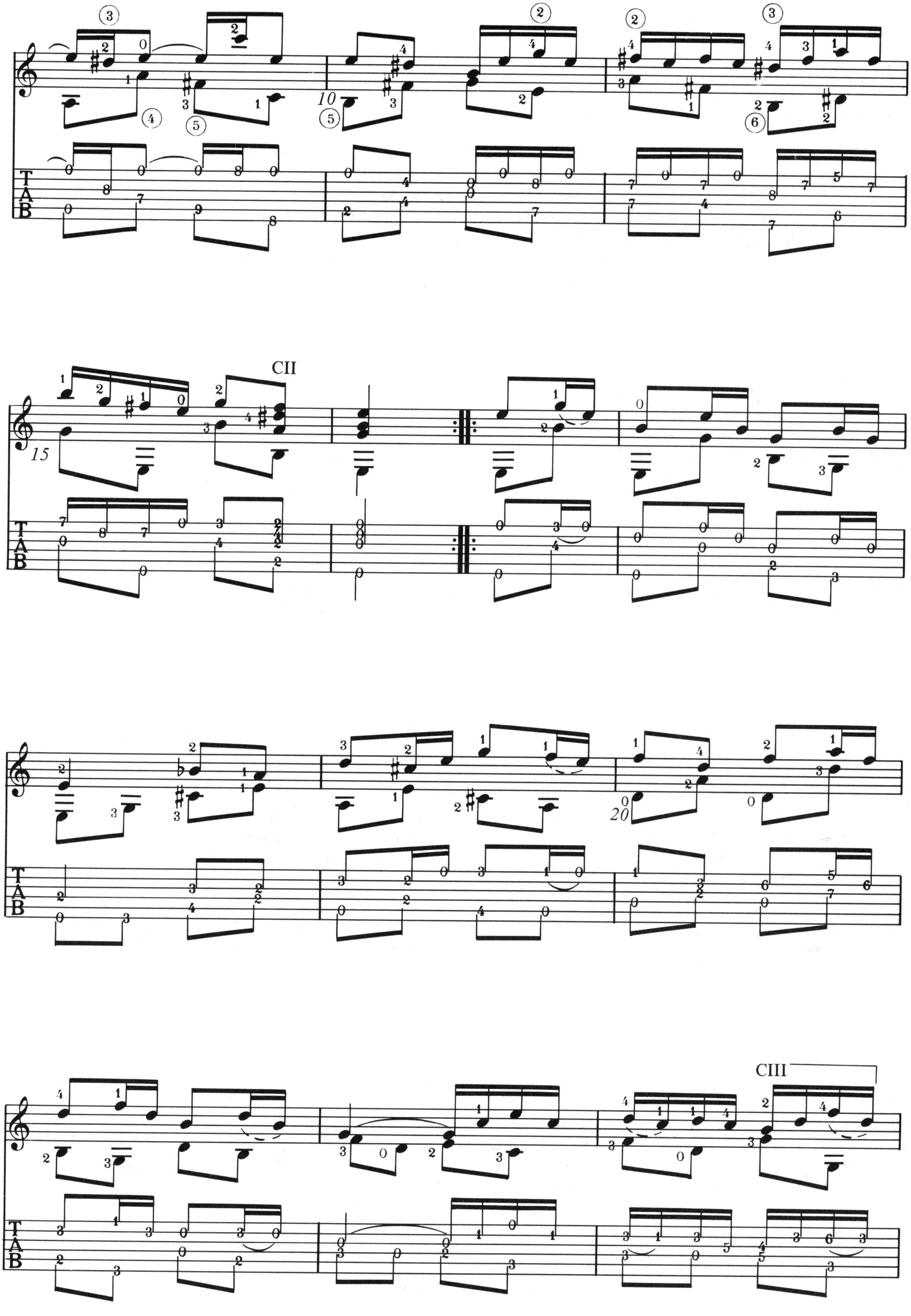
CII
CIII

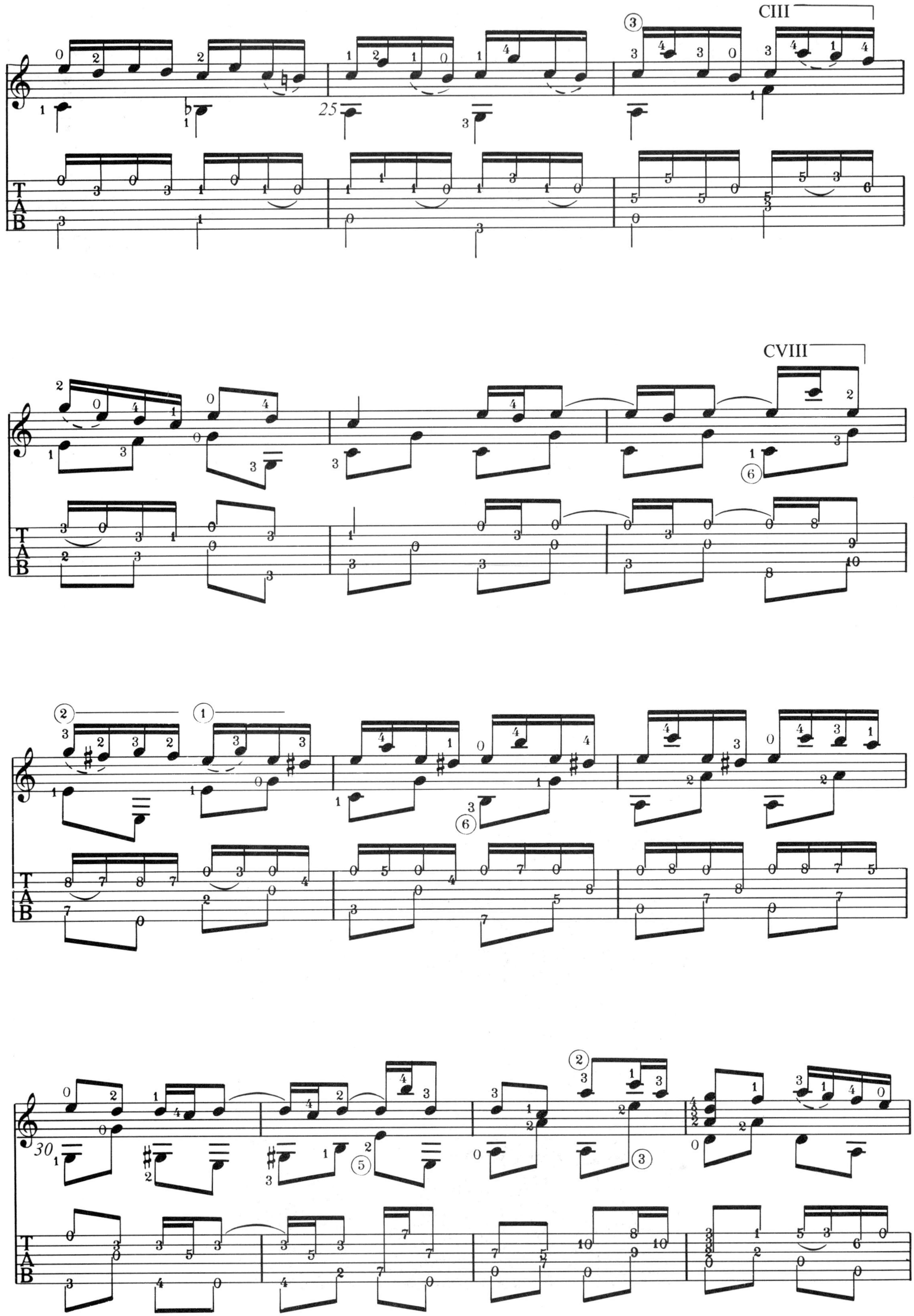
CIII
CVIII

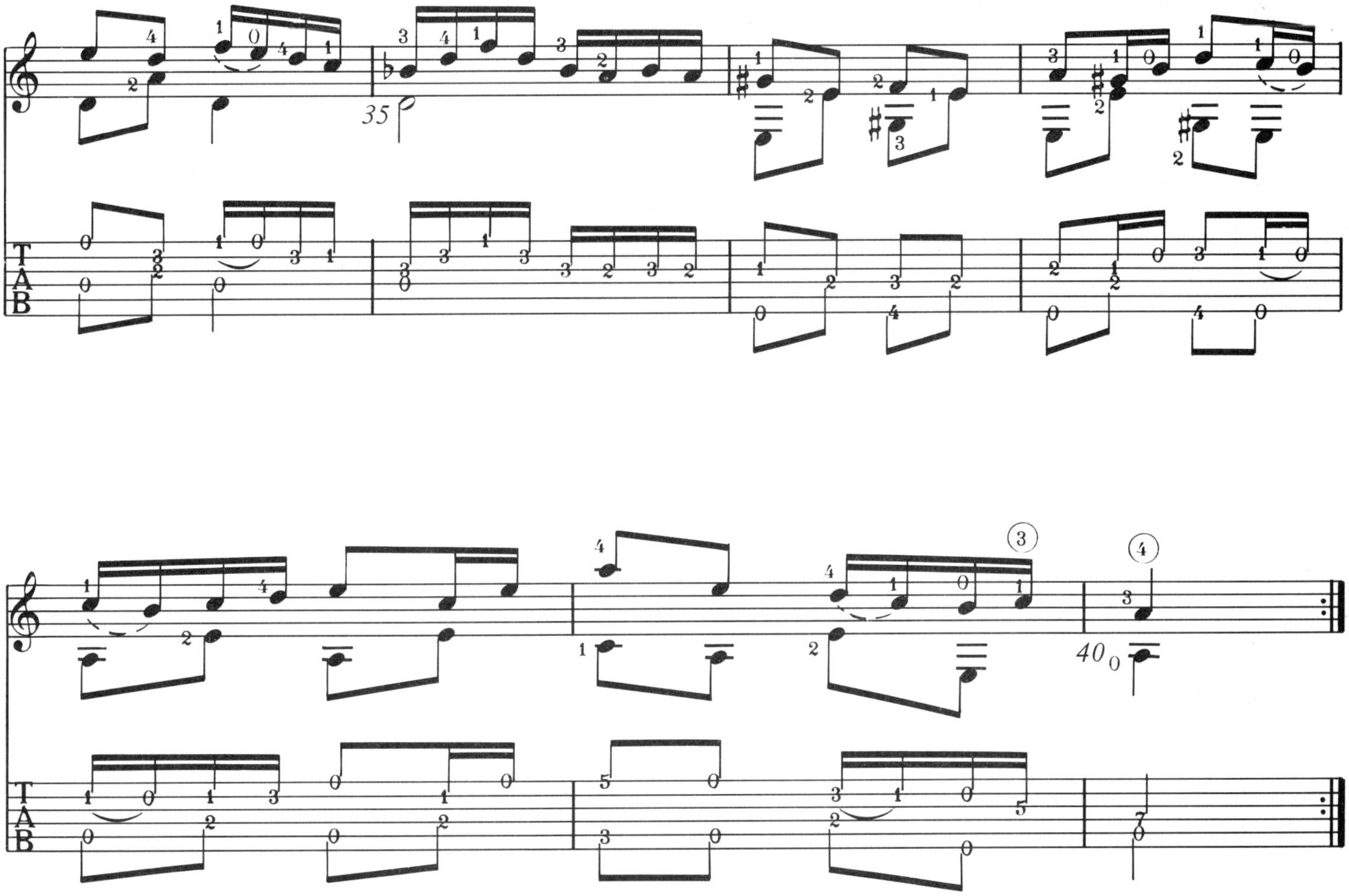
35
TAB
40
TAB

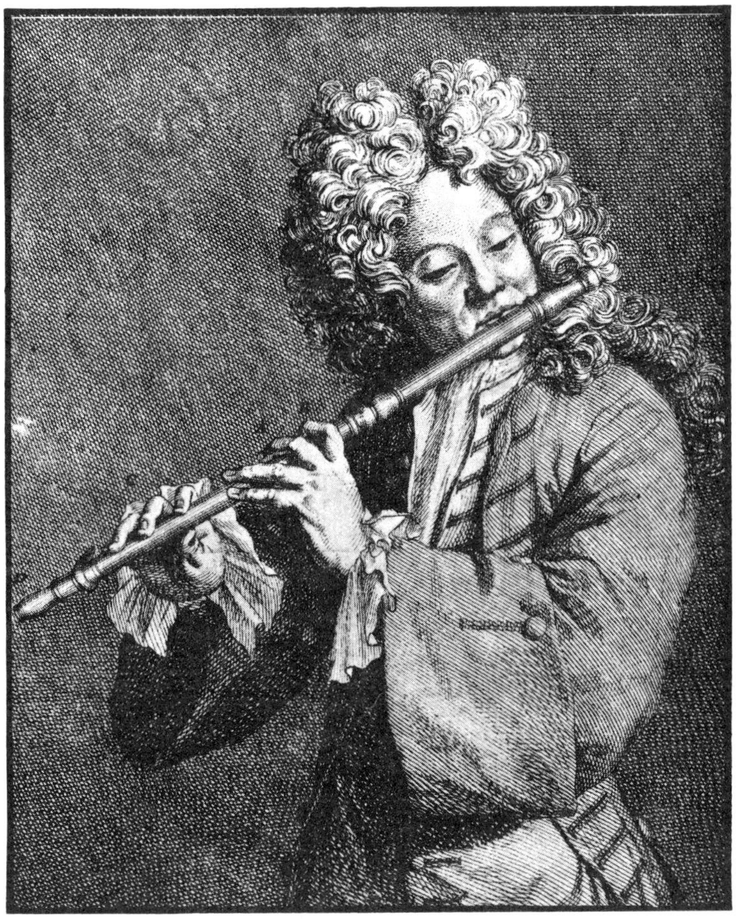